THE
LONG-DISTANCE
TEAM

ALSO BY KEVIN EIKENBERRY AND WAYNE TURMEL

The Long-Distance Leader: Rules for Remarkable Remote Leadership

The Long-Distance Teammate: Stay Engaged and Connected While Working Anywhere

THE
LONG-DISTANCE
TEAM

Designing Your Team for the Modern Workplace

KEVIN EIKENBERRY
AND WAYNE TURMEL

Berrett–Koehler Publishers, Inc.

Berrett-Koehler Publishers, Inc.
1333 Broadway, Suite 1000
Oakland, CA 94612-1921
Tel: (510) 817-2277
Fax: (510) 817-2278
www.bkconnection.com

ORDERING INFORMATION

Quantity sales. Special discounts are available on quantity purchases by corporations, associations, and others. For details, contact the "Special Sales Department" at the Berrett-Koehler address above.

Individual sales. Berrett-Koehler publications are available through most bookstores. They can also be ordered directly from Berrett-Koehler: Tel: (800) 929-2929; Fax: (802) 864-7626; www.bkconnection.com.

Orders for college textbook/course adoption use. Please contact Berrett-Koehler: Tel: (800) 929-2929; Fax: (802) 864-7626.

Distributed to the U.S. trade and internationally by Penguin Random House Publisher Services.

Berrett-Koehler and the BK logo are registered trademarks of Berrett-Koehler Publishers, Inc.

Printed in the United States of America.

Berrett-Koehler books are printed on long-lasting acid-free paper. When it is available, we choose paper that has been manufactured by environmentally responsible processes. These may include using trees grown in sustainable forests, incorporating recycled paper, minimizing chlorine in bleaching, or recycling the energy produced at the paper mill.

Library of Congress Cataloging-in-Publication Data
Names: Eikenberry, Kevin, 1962- author. | Turmel, Wayne, author.
Title: The long-distance team : designing your team for everyone's success
  / Kevin Eikenberry and Wayne Turmel.
Description: First Edition. | Oakland, CA : Berrett-Koehler Publishers,
  [2023] | Series: The long-distance worklife series | Includes
  bibliographical references and index.
Identifiers: LCCN 2022034202 (print) | LCCN 2022034203 (ebook) | ISBN
  9781523003419 (paperback) | ISBN 9781523003426 (pdf) | ISBN
  9781523003433 (epub) | ISBN 9781523003440
Subjects: LCSH: Virtual work teams. | Telecommuting. | Career development.
Classification: LCC HD66 .E35 2023 (print) | LCC HD66 (ebook) | DDC
  650.1—dc23/eng/20220919
LC record available at https://lccn.loc.gov/2022034202
LC ebook record available at https://lccn.loc.gov/2022034203

First Edition
30 29 28 27 26 25 24 23 22   10 9 8 7 6 5 4 3 2 1

Book producer and text designer: Happenstance Type-O-Rama
Cover designer: Adrian Morgan

*To our wives Lori and Joan who have
been our biggest supporters and fans for
a long time, and too often at a distance.*

To our wives Lori and Joan who have been our biggest supporters and fans for a long time, and too often at a distance.

Contents

Introduction   1

Part I   **Getting Started—Defining the Overused Terms**

    Chapter 1   What Is a Team, and Why Does It Matter?   9

    Chapter 2   What Is Culture?   17

Part II   **The Building Blocks**

    Chapter 3   Establishing Ownership of the Culture   25

    Chapter 4   Rethinking How We Work   39

    Chapter 5   The 3C Model for Team and Culture Design   47

Part III   **Designing for Success**

    Chapter 6   Designing Your Team   63

    Chapter 7   Redesigning an Existing Team   83

Part IV   **Creating Your Aspirational Culture**

    Chapter 8   Defining Your Aspirational Culture   93

    Chapter 9   Building the Micro Inside the Macro   105

    Chapter 10   Making the Culture Come to Life   113

Contents

Part V   Applying Core Principles

Chapter 11   **Applying the Power of Expectations**   127

Chapter 12   **Creating Team Agreements**   137

Chapter 13   **Creating Engagement**   147

Conclusion   159

Acknowledgments   163

Index   167

About the Authors   173

Helping Remote Leaders and Their Teams Succeed   175

Introduction

Work and how we all view it has changed drastically in the past few years.

When *The Long-Distance Leader* was released in 2018, the Covid-19 pandemic hadn't yet begun. *The Long-Distance Teammate* was published in January of 2021, nearly a year after a third of the workforce was suddenly working from home. We were told, "you were in the right place at the right time." We were, but it wasn't because of a pandemic. It was because, for nearly a decade, we had been looking at how work was changing and what it meant.

How and where we work was changing before the cataclysmic events of a pandemic. And although much is different, the biggest underlying factors about work haven't changed:

- There is still work to be done.

- Most of it is done with and for other people.

- Ninety-five percent of people want to do good and meaningful work 95 percent of the time.

- The key players are humans, who are both amazing and messy.

More than any of us can read has been written about work, working in teams, and getting those teams to get great results together. Most of those principles remain. But the context (where, when, and how people work) and our concept of work (how it fits into our life, and what we want work to look like) have changed greatly.

Let's be clear, this book is not "making teams work in a post-Covid world." In fact, as you read the book, you'll find few specific references to the global pandemic or its impact on teams. Partly this is an effort to make the book less restricted to a specific time in history and to maintain the big picture. But it's also because this shift didn't suddenly happen with the appearance of a specific virus. The way we work was already shifting under our feet. The events of the early 2020s simply made it clear to everyone (like it or not) that the old ways of thinking about our jobs and careers had already shifted. Those events simply put the need for us to reexamine some of our assumptions, behaviors, and decisions on fast-forward. We have much more to say about this new view of work later in Chapter 5, but this context sets the stage for this book.

Work, teams and teamwork, and the culture in which we do it all will remain important. Since all those things are changing, the way we think about, design around, and intentionally create those things must change too.

In the *Long-Distance Leader* we encouraged leaders to think "leadership first and location second." This is our way of saying not everything is new in your role—but what *is new* matters a whole lot. The same is true for this book. We will not take you through many of the things you know about traditional ways teams come together and help people work together successfully. Rather, we will help you intentionally design or redesign those teams in a world in which people may be working in different locations, at different times, and in different ways—and perhaps never (or rarely ever) see each other face to face.

In this context of a (rapidly) changing world of work, this book is about two important and overlapping factors: team design and culture.

What Are They and How Are They Different?

We will readily admit we have talked a lot about these two terms between ourselves and with clients, and often the words have been used interchangeably. Both are, in some ways, about how the work is done. However, we think there are important differences, and understanding the differences sets the stage for adjusting and applying both better in our working worlds. In short, we think of *team design* as how we organize around the nature of the work, and *culture* is how we do that work each day.

Let's be more specific.

Team Design

Team design is about framework, structure, and format. It is, at least at a high level, predefined (lots more about that to come). Team design addresses the what of the work, the why of the work, when the work is done, and by whom. How we intentionally design our teams needs to change, and we will help you do that through the ideas and practices in this book. It includes things like these:

- How we organize and define teams

- What reporting structures and connections between teams look like

- How team design is reflected in the policies about where and when people work and in job descriptions

In the past this has been determined by historical perspective, tradition, and accepted standards. It has been defined by boxes and organizational charts. With all the change swirling around us, tradition may be a good place to start, but overly relying on it doesn't serve us. Rather, team design (if your organization, team, or project is new) or redesign (if teams exist but could be more effective) should be dictated *by the needs of the work itself.*

Culture

Culture is about how we do our work and isn't about structure. Culture is more about daily behavior, the working environment, and how people feel when working. Culture is separate from team design because you could have very different structures and have similar cultures—or you could have similar structures and vastly different cultures. Culture doesn't have to be intentionally designed; it exists in every group of people. Where some external decisions and policies drive team design, culture naturally occurs as humans interact and adapt to each other. It includes things like these:

- Levels of engagement, accountability, and commitment

- The strength (or not) of relationships and trust

- How we deal with change

- The role of learning

- What we expect of/from each other

Culture always exists. There are pressures from some to take us back to a previous version and vision of culture—like it was some golden age. Successful organizations, teams, leaders, and individuals will intentionally seek an aspirational culture and want to work toward it. Creating and working toward an aspirational culture in this new world of work will create new, exciting results for everyone involved.

This book will help you do both—design or redesign your team and create and move toward the culture you want and need for everyone's success. We realize this isn't a one-time fix. Designing teams and refining culture is an ongoing process. We want to equip you for that journey.

You might be reading this thinking that team design and work and culture are enmeshed in ways that make it so you can't pull them apart. At the end of the day these concepts are interconnected. But for us to have highly effective teams and organizations that both get great work done and do it in ways that engage, enrich, and create enjoyment for those who do it, we must first separate these components.

We will intentionally look at the ideas of team design (or redesign) and culture development separately so that they can be joined in the real world in ways that create great synergy—even if the team operates at long distance.

We've written this book with your long-term success in mind. Some of the ideas are mentioned in our previous books. Although this book stands alone, the ideas in the others are necessarily connected to and support the ideas and actions in this book. Why? Because the basics of great teamwork and the challenges of working at a distance are consistent and apply no matter your formal position.

It doesn't matter if you are a senior leader, a mid-level manager, a front-line leader, or an individual who wants to help craft the environment in which you work. Ideas, questions, exercises, and resources are available throughout this book to help you design the team and culture you desire. When you do this work, you will be able to consistently create highly successful Long-Distance Teams.

Part I

Getting Started—
Defining the Overused Terms

Some words get overused in business books. The problem is that people all nod as if they understand them, either because they think they do or because they don't want people to think they are behind—or dense. When we get to this point, we need to step back and clarify what these words mean. In these first chapters we will do that to set the table for everything that follows.

Chapter 1

What Is a Team, and Why Does It Matter?

Kris has recently been promoted to project manager of a software development team that works remotely, mostly from home, across three countries. Several of the team members have worked together on past projects, but many are new to the company. She has six direct reports, but each works on their own tasks and seldom interacts with their teammates. Although the work gets done, she doesn't feel they are a team so much as a bunch of people who all work through her. Even though tasks are completed, and deadlines met, she wonders if there isn't something missing.

The last few years have changed how we work. When working from home exploded, a lot of leaders focused on just keeping the organization going. Can people meet deadlines and do good work when they aren't co-located? Will people put in the discretionary effort and communication efforts that have always been hallmarks of great teams? Can we keep the (figurative) doors open and stay in business until we go back to the office?

Those concerns were (and are) important, but they focused on imme-diate problems—putting out fires, as so many of us call it. Although it is easy to stay in fire-fighting mode, as leaders, we must put down the firehose and look to the future. When and where do people need to work to create great results? Can we collaborate effectively in new ways we haven't yet thought about? Although a two-year pandemic forced some of those ques-tions on us, we can't let the need to look forward and be proactive and intentional be a one-time pandemic-related response.

One of the most common questions we hear across organizations is this: "How do we create a 'one-team' workplace when we aren't in close proximity to each other all the time?"

Since you've invested in this book, you're probably at that stage your-self. You want a work environment that is more than individuals working for and answering to the same manager. Whether you're an individual con-tributor looking for the perfect workplace, a manager responsible for get-ting work done, or a senior leader charged with becoming an employer of choice, you have something in common. You want to be part of a high-per-forming, collaborative, innovative *team*. Whether you are leading a team that's been together for years, taking over an existing unit, or starting from scratch, you will be far more successful when you have considered answers to these questions:

- What kind of team is necessary to get the work done?

- What kind of team do you want to be part of?

- Can you create a team culture that meets those aspirations?

These questions are all important, and answering them is the focus of this book. But you can't really answer them without clearly defining one term.

What do we mean when we use the word, *team*?

Our old friend *Merriam-Webster* defines the word *team* this way:

1. A group of people who compete in a sport, game, etc., against another group

2. A group of people who work together to achieve a goal [for our purposes we can assume *together* doesn't have to mean physically]

3. A group of animals used to pull a wagon, cart, etc.

Assuming you aren't an athlete or an ox, definition two applies to most of us. Technically Kris, in the earlier story, has a team. All those smart programmers working on their tasks and answering to her are her *team*. But she (and likely you) feels like that isn't a satisfying answer. There must be more to being a great team than simply sharing a manager.

We agree.

A Quick Exercise

Take a blank sheet of paper and a pen. (You can use your computer or phone, but you'll likely get better results if you engage kinesthetically. Trust us.)

Set a timer for five minutes. When it starts, write down all the words, positive and negative, that you associate with the word *team*. When time is up, stop and look at the list. What words came to mind?

Everyone's lists will be different, but we have been doing this exercise for over twenty years and it's a good bet you included terms such as these:

- Helpful

- Aligned

- Collaborative

- Friendly (or at least collegial)

- Supportive

- Focused on the goal(s)

- More than the sum of its parts

You may also have included some words you might consider negative, such as these:

- Conflict

- Disagreement

- Inability to reach decisions

- Inefficient collaboration

Now stop and look at your list. If you are part of an existing team, which words reflect your current reality? We're betting that some of the traits you listed are present; after all, you've been together a while and work gets done. There are also features of a good team that you want—but aren't always experiencing.

Whether your team is brand new or has been together for a while, the overall process we will share is the same. Any time you have a gap between what you desire and what exists, you have room for improvement. We will take a deep dive into interpreting this exercise and turning it into action in the next few chapters.

An old Chinese proverb says, "The best time to plant a tree was twenty years ago. The second-best time is now." Whether your team has been together for years, or you're starting from scratch, it's always the right time to be intentional about what your team should, and can, look like.

In order to design a team, you first need to know what you want to achieve and recognize the circumstances under which that work happens.

Kevin has written and talked about two fundamentally different kinds of teams for years. We believe this distinction isn't considered often enough. The two types of teams are interdependent and independent teams; let's use a sports analogy to help us understand each.

Interdependent Teams

Basketball (or soccer or hockey) teams are *interdependent*. They require, by the nature of their work, that everyone play as one unit. On teams in these sports, the players rely on each other. At any moment of any game, to be successful, the entire team needs to be working in harmony. The role of each player is designated by their position (which considers their innate strengths and acquired skills). However, at any moment during the flow of the game, the situation may require any player to take any role, and use overlapping skills.

On successful teams of this sort, all players are willing to be flexible, to assist, to change roles, to "do what it takes," because they know that without working together, they can't achieve their team goals or victory—the nature of the game forces interdependency among the team members.

In the real world, an example is a customer service team in which people rely on the knowledge and experience of all their teammates to solve problems as quickly as possible, yet all can handle the emails and take the calls.

Independent Teams

Players on track-and-field teams, on the other hand (except in a few relay events), are part of an *independent* team. Shot putters have a skill set that is largely unrelated to the skills of sprinters. And the high jumpers can be personally skilled and successful without any tangible help or support from the distance runners. Sales teams are often independent in this way.

At the end of the day (or meet), if enough individuals win, the team wins. The most successful of these teams will have highly talented individual contributors supporting each other to reach their common goal of winning. In this way, they are surely a team. In the best cases they will feel allegiance and have pride in being a part of the group. They want each other to be successful. They know that they can all be more successful when each individual is more successful. They can have a common goal (to win the meet or championship). But the fundamental relationship between the players isn't the same as it is on a basketball/soccer/hockey team.

Why This Matters

In your organization you likely have both types of teams. You have teams that work in a process flow or project where the outputs of one person directly affect the work of the next, where the work and the people are highly interdependent. In other situations, people work toward a common mission and goal, but their work doesn't intersect in nearly the same ways as for the highly interdependent teams.

This difference matters because in our experience, and in most of the conversation surrounding Long-Distance Teams, people assume we have and desire interdependent teams. If the work or project dictates that focus, great. But if you have a track-and-field (independent) team, you don't need the same focus on interdependence and traditional team-building activities nor the same needs for interaction and collaboration.

If you lead, form, or are a part of teams, you need to think about this distinction. We will help you with it throughout the book. Once you determine the type of team you want and need, you can set appropriate and effective expectations and design accordingly.

Finally, a Definition

For simplicity, let's define a great team this way:

A group of people working together to achieve their common goals through an intentional culture, positive energy, collaboration, innovation, and human connection.

So, a Long-Distance Team is this:

A group of people working together to achieve their common goals through an intentional culture, positive energy, collaboration, innovation, and human connection, regardless of their physical location.

While we're at it, we should probably get specific about some terminology we will associate with teams. Our definition applies whether people work in a common location or not. All teams operate in similar ways, but Long-Distance Teams vary in form, and there are subtle differences between them, which we'll discuss as we go.

For now, let's think about them in three forms:

- **Remote Teams:** Teams whose members do not share a common workspace. They may work from home or from third spaces such as remote offices, but seldom do they see each other in person and they communicate almost entirely through technology.

- **Hybrid Teams:** Some team members work in a central location or office, whereas others are remote, some or all the time. In essence, nobody is co-located all the time. There are endless combinations, and all of them have nuances and challenges to consider.

- **Flexible Teams:** The nature of the work may dictate that there are no hard-and-fast rules for who works where, and when. On any given day, people may be in the office or not.

None of these types is "right," but one is right for you and the team you want to design. This book will help you think about all those options and variables.

Now that we've defined what a team is, let's talk about the kind of team you want to have. Let's talk about culture.

Chapter 2

What Is Culture?

Julia tries to be well read on leadership. She attributes her relatively fast rise in the organization to her diligence and discipline in understanding how to lead and apply the concepts around leadership. Culture is one of those topics she's read about. And although many topics have become clearer to her, some others—like culture—remain a bit of a mystery. She is still trying to understand how culture relates to her daily work and what she as a leader can do to leverage that knowledge for the good of her team and organization.

Some words, including *culture*, become buzzwords. They become jargon because they are important and/or many people are interested in the idea. As they become overused, they lose most of their meaning. That is how Julia feels—she is smart and willing to learn, yet, when the word *culture* comes up in a meeting, she smiles and nods knowingly like everyone else.

Julia isn't alone. For most people this word isn't completely clear and has been overly complicated. We aim to change that right now.

Have you ever been walking on a trail in the woods? If so, you know that although you can see the trees in front of you, it is hard to describe the whole forest. At that moment, the forest for you is the trees—because you just see the trees around you. Patterns, dimension, and a bigger perspective are hard to recognize when all you see are . . . trees.

Culture is a bit like that. You go to work every day and just see the work. Over time, you realize certain norms or approaches are just accepted facts; they are "how we do work around here." If you have worked more than one place, you might start to see the differences from one place to the next, and if so, you are starting to "see" what culture means.

Culture?

Although the concept is simple and all around us, let's define and give some examples of culture and then share some other important points about it. Culture is . . .

- *How we do things around here.* This is our simplest definition. If you want to be successful quickly in a new job, find a person who can help you understand this. It is about more than the policies and procedures. The things that are written down and say something about the beliefs of the organization are important, but the things not written down are even more powerful. It's one thing for the training and procedures to say, "We return customer emails within the business day," but when do they really get answered? A team's culture includes the unwritten rules and norms as well as the political dynamics between people, both helpful and less-so.

- *The stories we are told (and retell).* If the stories you hear repeated officially and unofficially in the organization are about heroic actions of employees to serve customers, that says something about the way the company values customer service. If you hear stories about product shipping regardless of the standards, because "we have to make our numbers," that says something too. There are stories in every organization and their messages become a part of the culture. Oh, and what do we do when we hear a story? Tell it to someone else. And the culture deepens.

- *The behaviors that get you promoted.* Do people get promoted because they are ruthless in pursuit of personal status and glory? Are people promoted because of tenure or length of service because loyalty is a company value? Or are people promoted because they have the ability to do the next job? The behaviors that lead to promotion—that define success—are an embedded part of the culture. The *perceptions* of which behaviors get you promoted are at least as important as the reality.

- *The stuff that gets recognized.* The things that are mentioned in the company newsletter, or in the quarterly all-hands meeting, or that get recognized in your performance review matter. If those clues all mention individual accomplishment or effort, that likely overrides all the "team talk" on the website or in the values statements.

- *The values the organization lives by.* Most organizations of any size or age have a stated set of values. They are on the wall in the conference room, discussed in orientation and onboarding processes, and posted proudly on websites. These are a part of the culture, but only to the degree that they are lived.

Stories, examples, and personal observation define the true values, regardless of what is written down. And these values-in-action are a cornerstone of your organizational culture.

Beyond these definitional descriptions, here some other truths about culture. Culture is . . .

- *Everywhere.* There is no such thing as an organization, group, team, or family that doesn't have a culture. You know what happens at your family gatherings and holidays, what food will be served, and much more. We often call this tradition, but it is culture—how we do things around here. If you go to a similar gathering of a different family, you might feel disoriented and mildly uncomfortable; some of those feelings come from the differences in culture.

- *Naturally occurring.* Just as there is no forest without trees, there is no culture without people. But as soon as people show up, they start feeling each other out and determining the unwritten ways things will be done. People bring their values, personalities, tendencies, and past experiences, and all those mesh to create a culture where one didn't exist previously.

- *Always changing.* When circumstances, players, environment, or context change, culture shifts. When someone gets married and starts attending the family gathering, the culture changes a little. When someone brings a new dish to the holiday dinner, and then brings it a second time, it is now expected. Although many of these changes might be small, even imperceptible at first, it is important to realize that culture can and does change.

- *Not out of our control.* This is important! Although culture will shift and change naturally, just as it forms without planning, it can be altered, improved, and adjusted. In a world of work that keeps changing, we can do things to adjust and create the culture we want and need. This is one of the keys to the future success of your team and organization.

The Layers of Culture

Kevin grew up in western Michigan about ten miles east of Lake Michigan. That massive body of water changes the local climate in all seasons of the year. The climate at the lakeshore is different than at his farm—in summer it is cooler near the lake and warmer at the farm. In winter the opposite can be true. And the further from Lake Michigan you get, the more that difference materializes. There are even further differences within a field—between hills and low spots.

So, while there is a Mason County, Michigan, climate, there are also microclimates based on the specific location—many of them. None of those microclimates is completely different from the macroclimate of Mason County, Michigan, which is significantly different than that of Mason County, Washington (near Seattle).

Similarly, your organization has multiple cultures. Specifically let's say there are two types:

Macroculture: The cultural norms of the larger organization. This is based on the beliefs, experience, traditions, and history of the organization.

Microculture: The cultural norms, behaviors, and expectations of an individual team. This is the culture we feel and experience each day.

Much like our climate example, the microculture fits inside the macroculture but can be significantly different. And there can be multiple microcultures across teams, divisions, countries, and more. We discuss all of this more in Chapter 9.

Final Thoughts

Culture matters because although it is invisible most of the time, it is powerful and pervasive. We consider culture to be a big invisible lever that moves our organization/team and impacts productivity, retention, customer satisfaction—almost everything. Once you see the lever, you can begin to adjust it and move your organization in new directions. Archimedes said, "Give me a lever long enough and a fulcrum on which to place it, and I shall move the world." You don't need to move the world, just your organization. Once you understand what culture is, you have the lever to create that movement.

But where does culture come from? Who gets to decide what the culture is and what is (and isn't) part of the way things get done? Who makes the rules? The answer is simple—everyone who is part of the culture. How we make that happen is more complex. We'll go there next.

Part II

The Building Blocks

To get to "the modern workplace" we promise in the subtitle, we must consider some key things first, including ownership, and creating a clear picture of what work will look like before we design. We will discuss those things and introduce the 3C Model, which will guide your thinking and efforts through the rest of the book.

Chapter 3

Establishing Ownership of the Culture

Cho is not sure he's landed the right job. When he interviewed with the project manager, the work sounded fast-paced, high energy, and fun. But now that he's got the job, everything seems to take a long time. Decisions from other parts of the organization take forever, and often they contradict what the project team is trying to accomplish. Internal communication is much more formal than he is used to. It seems like the macroculture of the company is very different from the microculture on the team. Whose job is it to determine the company's culture: the team's or the company's? And what's he supposed to do?

Who Owns Culture?

We've already established that a simple definition of culture is "how things are done around here."

Says who?

Did the senior leadership sit around a table and decide, "we want to be really bureaucratic and methodical about how we operate"? Does the manager putting together a new team send a memo stating, "Okay, starting Thursday, we're going to be fun and not afraid to take chances"? When new people join the team, do they sacrifice their personality and workstyle to match the existing culture so they fit in seamlessly and keep the culture exactly as it was?

It can often seem as though nobody is really in charge of creating the culture; it merely evolves and morphs over time. That certainly can happen—and it does, often, which is why so many of us are dissatisfied with the way things are done on our teams.

One of the primary purposes of this book is to help you dream up, design, and take specific steps to create the kind of culture that will be best for the work you do and the people you do it with. But who is ultimately responsible for that culture? Who decides how things should be, and more importantly, who gets to put the metrics and processes in place to ensure those aspirations are met?

Is how we work decided by the most senior leaders? By those at the team level? Or is it determined by each of us individually, as demonstrated by how we do our jobs every day?

Senior leaders, line managers, and everyone else all contribute to both the macroculture and microculture of our organization. Because we contribute, we are also partly responsible. So, who owns the creation of a team's culture?

The Role of Senior Leadership

If you are a senior leader, you already know you have a part to play in what it's like to work in and be part of that organization. People take their behavior cues from those above them on the org chart. Your people watch how you go about your work and hope to receive guidance from you on how to conduct business. They might even read and pay attention to the lovely mission and vision statements the company issues.

There's a paradox here. Although you may have incredible influence in setting policy, you aren't doing much of the day-to-day work. You're not dealing with customers and getting product out the door. That's where the microculture gets shaped and solidified.

In the popular TV series, *Undercover Boss*, CEOs disguise themselves to work on the front lines of the businesses. Inevitably, they learn that the workaday reality of the job looks very different from their assumptions. It's easy to blame them for being "out of touch," or "up in their ivory towers while we do the real work." But why is there this disconnect?

It's not that most senior leaders don't care. It's that they have a completely different job than the person fulfilling orders in the warehouse, so they have a different perspective and experience.

Sometimes this is a result of history. If you are the founder of a business, odds are the culture stems directly from how you operated at the start. Let's get really personal for a moment and give you an example from our own business.

Like so many businesses, The Kevin Eikenberry Group started with Kevin. There was no "group," just Kevin working from a desk in his extra bedroom trying to get his company off the ground. He didn't set out to create a culture; he literally was the culture. Every decision, from what the workbooks looked like to what color the business cards and logos were, to which organizations he marketed to, reflected his personality, ethics, preferences, and workstyle. As the company grew and the team grew, he was able to choose those team members he felt would be a good fit, so even as his organization got bigger, the way things were done still reflected his personality.

Now it's more than twenty-five years later. Although the company with his name on it continues to do business, and he's very involved, he doesn't and shouldn't (and can't) do all the work himself. He has a sales team who interacts with customers that Kevin will probably never meet or talk to. Although he has input into what's taught in workshops, he's not always delivering the learning himself and often has only an indirect role in the design of some of our solutions.

Beyond being the coauthor of this book, Wayne has an important role to play in the organization. As product manager for the Long-Distance Leadership part of the business, his workstyle is very different from Kevin's and their work reflects those personality differences. Wayne is less systems-driven and more spontaneous. He has a wackier sense of humor and comes across as brash and extroverted, whereas Kevin seems calmer and more methodical.

Over the years, the additions to the team have changed the culture. This isn't a bad thing. We are aligned on what it means to do business with us. Collectively we have created a common vision. We have similar beliefs in how to work with customers and about the importance of our work, and we have a common commitment to the quality of that work and how we treat our teammates. We just go about it in different ways than what Kevin did when he worked alone in the spare room.

If you're a senior leader at an established organization, a culture existed when you arrived. If you came up through the ranks, you might be more comfortable and familiar with how things are done—after all, you helped form it. If you've joined from outside the company, you may still be trying to understand how people work together to make the business hum.

Just as Kevin learned as his company grew, senior leaders can have a great influence on the culture of an organization, but much less direct control. They can recruit people who are a good fit, brainstorm vision and mission statements to guide decision-making, and market to the public in a way that fits the brand—and getting this right is the senior leader's job.

When two or three people get together to create a customer solution, they are going to work in their own way and come up with solutions the leader might not have thought of or know about. The more those decisions get made without input or oversight from the leader, the more the microculture of that team will differ from the macroculture of the company.

If they can't directly control the culture, what is senior leadership's role?

- To create space for culture to be intentionally improved (there's lots more on this later in the book)

- To communicate the culture and values internally and externally

- To create processes in place to support and reinforce desired behaviors

- To model the attitudes and behaviors they expect throughout the organization

Communicating the Company Culture and Values

When you are a leader, people look to you for guidance on how things should be done. As your organization expands, individuals have less exposure to the company as a whole and tend to focus on the work of their team or business unit. Marketing, Engineering, and Sales often work in very different ways. One thing that unites them is they work for your organization, and "there's a way we do things here."

Only senior leaders have both ethical and positional authority over all the parts of the organization. If you want everyone to share values and behaviors, they need to hear a consistent message and know that message (and those behaviors) will be rewarded and reinforced.

Putting Processes and Systems in Place to Support Culture

How you recruit the right people, train them to work in the right way, and recognize and reward the behaviors your company values are all important to senior leadership. Does the way people work every day reflect what they say they want as an organization?

Wayne dealt with an example of this early in his career. He worked for a family-owned car dealership in Southern California. The management spent a lot of time talking about how they were different from other dealerships, because they "worked as a family," and "helped each other out to do what's right for the customer." Yet sales were recorded on a white board, with each individual rep's daily tally up there for all the world to see. Compensation was purely based on individual sales. Helping a coworker who was having trouble closing a sale (usually Wayne) only meant that person would get the money and you'd have lost the chance to make a sale of your own. The desired culture (cooperation and teamwork) was undermined by the system.

Although the owners legitimately wanted to create a culture of teamwork, the primary system—in this case compensation—rewarded people for handling their own business at the expense of their peers.

There are many more examples of this principle than compensation, yet we use this example because it is a common point of misalignment between desired/stated culture and actual results.

If retaining good people is important to you, does the way your company trains and rewards new employees encourage a "churn and burn" approach to staffing? This is just another example of the role of senior leaders in the real work and outcomes.

Senior Leaders Need to Model the Culture

How is senior leadership viewed by the rest of the organization? Do they "walk the talk"? A simple example is how failure is seen and talked about. If you want a culture of innovation, there will be mistakes—some costly. If your culture is focused on excellence of execution, there will be less tolerance for errors. Perfection is the point.

How do leaders in your organization talk about failure? Does it match what you want? What is the process for debriefing products and capturing lessons learned? Are people afraid to speak up or take chances because they're worried about losing their jobs?

Making Space for Improving the Culture

Senior leaders are busy, often so busy they don't take time to ask how things are going. Even if they are mindful of their responsibility and impact on the culture, they don't have visibility to every part of the organization. Often, they are blissfully unaware of the organization's microcultures.

They need to recognize that assessing and taking stock of culture is not a one-time event but a process. Incorporating assessment tools like NPS (Net Promoter Score), gathering ongoing feedback across the organization, and taking exit interviews seriously are good examples. That's why we encourage senior leaders to regularly consider these two questions:

- What kind of macroculture does your company claim to have?

- How well do your daily leadership behaviors communicate, reflect, and support those behaviors?

The Role of the Team Leader

Most of the work in an organization gets done at the team level. On a day-to-day basis, we as team leaders have very specific goals to be met and tasks that must be done. Unlike senior leaders, we work with the same people in our teams every day. That constant interaction helps create and reinforce our team's microculture.

There is a hard truth about leading teams. The old adage, "people don't quit jobs, they quit managers," is true. The number one reason people leave their teams or organizations is because of their relationship with their leader and the way they lead. Although team leaders are not responsible for every factor in their team culture, they own more than they often realize.

Team leaders, project managers, and managers own a lot of the culture, including

- Being the main connection and conduit between the team and the organization's macroculture

- Being responsible for helping new people adapt and fit in to the way the team works

- Modeling the behaviors and attitudes that create the desired culture

When you look at these three roles, it is hard to argue against the importance of team leaders/supervisors/middle managers in creating and nurturing culture.

The Connection between the Organization and the Team

Although there are a lot of unkind jokes about middle management, their role is critical. They connect the larger organization to the team. Information flows through them both ways. Among other responsibilities, they must communicate news and information that explains and supports the vision.

Anyone in a leadership/management role, regardless of title, is a "manager in the middle." One of the hardest things about being in this situation is that they are on (at least) two teams—the team they lead and the team of their peers. This often leaves them walking the line between responsibility to the direct team and being an ambassador/advocate for the entire organization.

They must help people understand and apply the systems, whether they are recognition programs, performance management processes, or any of dozens of others that are put in place to support the macroculture. That can be uncomfortable when there's a disconnect between what the organization says they want and the reality of the daily work.

When there isn't a big disparity between macro- and microcultures, there's no problem. If a disparity exists, it is confusing at a minimum, and often it's a significant problem. If compensation or recognition encourages individual accomplishment when the culture purportedly celebrates team-work, which wins in the real world?

Bringing New People into the Team

The existing team has a culture. Every new person you bring in will create a variation in that team dynamic—whether positive or otherwise. One of the most important responsibilities of a team leader is to help new people acclimate as quickly as possible to their work and the culture and start adding value to the team's work.

When they have direct responsibility for hiring, they are responsible for bringing in the right people. This doesn't mean each of these team members has to be an exact cultural fit. Hiring for "perfect fit" can be a recipe for groupthink and doesn't allow the team to achieve diversity of thought and experience that can help them become more effective. Although finding the perfect fit might not be their goal, leaders must help people acclimate to the culture and guide and coach new members to help them in their transition.

This doesn't just happen when a leader brings someone on board, points to a desk, or gives them the network log-on information. Leaders set the tone and help people understand the dynamics at work on the team. They also set expectations about not just the work to be done, but how it is to be done, and by whom. The existing teammates play a role in helping the new hire adjust and understand both the spoken and unspoken ways "we do things here."

Everyone who joins a team affects the culture. When we are intentional about introducing and supporting the team behavior, it's more likely we'll end up with employees who are a good cultural fit as the team is currently constructed and who own their part in creating what comes next.

Modeling the Culturally Appropriate Behaviors

Few things impact the culture as much as the team leader's day-to-day behavior. You can say you want a team that is empowered to make decisions, but why must everything be run through you for approval? You want to get innovative and think outside the box to get the best possible results, yet you are constantly coaching people to play nicely and go along to get along.

Your team takes their cues from you. If you don't take your assigned personal time off days, or PTO, or you answer and send emails at all hours of the day and night, what makes you think your people will respect their own work-life balance? What you say is not nearly as important as how you behave day in and day out.

And this applies on a Long-Distance Team as well—just because they can't "see" you doesn't mean they aren't watching.

The Role of the Individual

As an individual, you might feel powerless, but you aren't. Here is some truth for you:

- You must recognize the culture in which you work.
- You are responsible for your behavior even though you can't control what others do.
- You have more influence than you think.

Recognize the Culture in Which You Work

One of Wayne's favorite quotes is from Marshall McLuhan: "I don't know who discovered water, but it wasn't a fish." That's a roundabout way of saying that, too often, we are so immersed in our surroundings that we don't stop to recognize where we are or what's going on around us.

When we don't question or pay attention to "how things work around here," we can find ourselves going through the motions—doing the same things in the same way all the time. This isn't bad when these things are the right behaviors. When we work intentionally, and not on autopilot, we can see if the behaviors are a problem.

To constantly improve (more on this later), both individually and as a team, you must assess and question your team's culture. Once you understand what is going on, it is easy to ask why something is done that way and whether things need to be adjusted or changed.

It all starts with recognizing the nature of the water you're in.

You're Responsible for Your Behavior

As a team member, you are a component in the culture. How you do your work, communicate with others, and meet your responsibilities is your contribution to how your team gets things done. Your actions are all part of the culture of your team.

No matter how routine your job might be, you are not just a cog in the machine with no control. Every time you send an email, choose to ignore a request for help, or volunteer for a project, you've made a decision that has an impact.

When you understand and recognize the culture you work in, it becomes clear how important your choices become. For example, let's say your workplace culture is based on harmony and getting along more than on the quality of results. That might be good or bad, depending on the quality of the decisions you all make, but that's how things work there. Since you are deciding how you work, you have three options: you can shrug your shoulders and just go along with everyone, knowing the results won't be optimum; you can suggest a change in a way that will be acceptable to the team and that doesn't rock the boat, knowing it might not be accepted; or you can pound your fist on the table out of frustration, pushing your idea and upsetting some team members.

Your response is a choice—you can choose whether to be passive, aggressive, or more carefully communicate. By knowing the water you are swimming in, you can make better choices as to how things get done.

You Have More Influence Than You Think

A culture existed when you arrived and will be there after you leave. That doesn't mean things are unchangeable—in fact culture is always changing in small ways. When you have a clear picture of how things work, you can decide how to make it better.

Do you like how things work? Keep working in ways that support those things.

Do some things feel wrong, or do you see how they could be better for everyone? Maybe you see that team members are unwilling to help each other out or that the team lacks urgency when working with other departments. Maybe cliques are forming with the people who are in the office on the same days. You can choose to go along, deciding that these issues are not worth fighting about or that you don't see how to change things. Or you might decide that your conscience bothers you so you're going to work in a way that makes you feel better about the work you do.

In co-located workplaces, these problems arise, and the impact is felt immediately. In many cases you can feel tensions rising and see the look on people's faces and realize "someone" should do something about it. When we work remotely, however, or as part of the hybrid team, such reactions and initial tension are invisible and people are unaware of what's happening, so it takes longer to recognize the problem. That's why people may be less prone to take immediate action in such situations (which make matters worse than was necessary).

When we aren't all together, there is a lot of "whitespace" between taking action and seeing the results. If we don't intentionally examine those gaps in our awareness and knowledge, we create more room for misunderstandings and bad assumptions, and team cohesion can suffer.

Everyone—those with leadership titles and positions or not—is accountable for their role in maintaining the culture and the part they'll play in its evolution over time.

The choices you make will certainly impact your work—and everyone else's too. You may feel better about your work if you put more effort into helping your teammates. Or you might feel awful by just going along with the way things have always been done. But deciding to change your behavior for the right reasons can have a positive ripple effect.

We have experienced the same challenges. For example, some members of our team used to send emails requesting assistance without clarifying the timeframe for their request. Such requests sometimes caused people to become confused and frustrated as people stopped one task to assist, only to find out later there was no hurry. By being clear about time expectations (putting the timeframe for the request in the subject line or the first line of the email), we began to have fewer useless "fire drills" and demonstrated more respect for each other's time. Kevin is happy for the greater productivity too.

Raise the issue you see that others might not have seen. Suggest changes in a way that your team culture will support. Act in a way that respects your own values and ethics. You'll be surprised at the impact it will have on the team.

Final Thoughts

Wherever you sit, recognize that you have an important role to play in your team's microculture. Every decision, conversation, and action plays a part in your evolving culture. Pointing the finger elsewhere doesn't help—and doing so dampens the levels of accountability and responsibility in your culture. If you didn't realize it before, we hope that you see it now.

Chapter 4

Rethinking How We Work

Malcolm has had a long, and by most all measures, successful career. He mastered the mechanics of the workplace and learned how to lead effective meetings and drive results. As people were forced to work from home, and they began requesting (though it felt like demanding to him) to work remotely, he became uncomfortable. What used to be the accepted norm now feels like choppy water. Part of him wants to change, adapt, and start swimming, but part of him—a big part—feels completely out of his element. He wants the model and mechanics he has known and worked to master his whole adult life and wonders if that is even possible anymore.

Malcolm is like a lot of leaders we've met and worked with. They're uncomfortable with a future of work that they aren't used to—and haven't been successful in. It's crucial that we understand their motivation and see them as more than just an out-of-touch, I-want-everyone-in-the-office stubborn leader.

How they feel and what they see makes sense when you look at their experience and past success. If Malcolm has been part of successful teams and attributed the organization's (and his personal) success to the way things were done, he sees changes as likely threats. To go back to the fish analogy, he only knows the water he has swum in his whole life—and he has been successful in it. All that points him (and all the Malcolms in the world) to a traditional, in-person workplace. Many leaders have no experience with remote work themselves and try to make hybrid work mirror the traditional office as much as possible.

The trepidation makes perfect sense. Inaction does not.

How We View Work

Even if we aren't as seasoned as Malcolm, we have much in common with others in how we view work and how it gets done. Some of this is ingrained and we don't even think about it. Take for example, the nine-to-five, forty-hour work week. For most of us, work is framed around those forty hours. And even if we do shift work, or work in service industries where we might work weekends, we accept—and our language tells us—that Monday through Friday is the "work week."

But that pattern didn't always exist. Before the 1920s when Henry Ford and his contemporaries adopted the assembly line and the standards that came with it, most people who didn't work on a farm or in a family business worked six days a week, and ten or more hours day. That was their reality, just like nine-to-five, forty hours per week has been ours. In fact, although there had been much testing and discussion about an eight-hour day as early as the 1860s, the forty-hour week didn't become a standard in the United States until the Great Depression, when the government saw a forty-hour week as a way to spread the work between more people and reduce unemployment. By 1940 laws had enshrined the forty-hour work week as the norm.

Knowledge work has some assumptions built into it too. They are rooted in the post–World War II boom in office work, and a lot of assumptions haven't changed. We meet in conference rooms, brainstorm in groups, have coffee-room, water-cooler, and hallway conversations. We go to lunch together. We work *together*, in close proximity. People come to the office at a certain time, and for the most part, there is a common quitting time. So much about how we see work is based in these traditions and patterns.

This worldview of work served us well for a time and is fine in a static world. But static doesn't describe the world today.

How It Has Changed

Our point isn't that our past model was right, simply that we have unconsciously accepted it as the standard. It hasn't been in place forever, yet it still defines "work" (and not just for Malcolm). In fact, in our working lives, there have been experiments and deviations. Some people work four tens (including Kevin's wife Lori)—stuffing forty hours into four days a week. And Kevin left Chevron in 1993, where they had already been applying a nine-eighty schedule (work your eighty hours in nine days rather than ten) for several years. Although both these models exist, neither has become the norm, and more importantly, both are still rooted in the five days, forty common hours model. Several countries in the EU are trying out a four-day work week—thirty-two hours a week for the same pay. A lot of people are merely tinkering with the formula.

What's Our Point?

Simply stated, the world and the world of work have changed. The trend toward a more flexible and remote working model has existed for many years. The pandemic, and its results, have put that trend into hyperdrive. When so much of the working world had an extended experience with working remotely (and everyone else knew or lived with someone who did and wanted to try it themselves), we put the future on fast forward.

In the big picture—we had eighty years to talk about moving down to eight hours of work per day, then eighty years of us living in that reality. Now we aren't just looking at how many hours we work, but where we work, when we do that work, who we work with, and how work gets done.

Everything has changed in, historically, the blink of an eye. When we look back today, we might assume things transitioned smoothly. Trust us, it didn't, and we are living that next very bumpy transition now.

It is no wonder people are stressed, worried, and longing for "the good old days" when they knew what work looked like.

Getting Everyone on the Same (New) Page

Part of the message of this book, is that we are all—leaders at all levels and teammates of all stripes—in this together. For us to determine our best team structures, working arrangements, culture, and view of work, we must come together and decide together. This book is meant to help everyone get on that same page. This chapter is meant to give you some perspective on why doing so is important and why it may seem so hard.

Let's look at all the variables that are set or assumed in the current—postindustrial—world of work:

- *Where we will work.* This is the one most people think about first, and admittedly, what for some feels like the biggest change in paradigm of work. The options here are many. Will we all be together some or all the time? Will some people "never" come to the office? Will geographical location matter at all?

- *When we will work.* When we will work relates to days in the week, times of the day, and overall hours in the week. What do we want, and what will allow the work outputs and goals to be reached?

- *How we will work.* This is a big part of this book. We need to determine the work processes and culture—from how we design the team, to the work processes, the culture, and more. We have more decisions to make here than ever before—even though they are as obvious as the other decisions we discussed.

- *Who we will work with.* Who will be on the team and how do we define team? What will be our goals and desires around diversity of all sorts? How will we think about part-timers, contract/gig employees, and more? Where are people from, and what are their backgrounds and perspectives?

What Can't Be Forgotten

In *The Long-Distance Leader* we introduced the Three O Model of Leadership. We shared this model to give a framework for thinking about the nature of the leader's role.

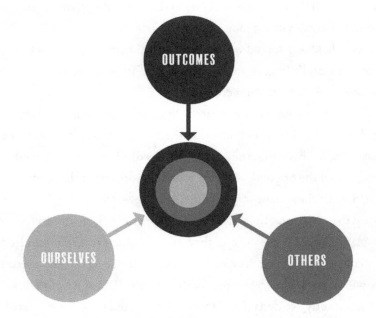

Figure 1: The Three O Model. Copyright Kevin Eikenberry Group.

Look at the space between the Outcomes and Others circles in Figure 1. Much of the discussion and decisions, the chaos, and the challenges we are facing as we look to the future are about balance between getting the organizational goals and objectives (Outcomes) we need and meeting the needs and expectations of the team (Others). The needs of both Outcomes and Others must be constantly balanced and considered. If we just think about what team members need and want without the context and meaning of the organizational outcomes (or alternatively, we focus solely on the organizational needs, ignoring the needs of the team), we will make incomplete decisions with unintended consequences.

The Lesson of Hybrids

Way back in 2017, we started talking about *hybrid teams*. Although we wish we could claim credit for that phrase becoming a permanent part of our lexicon, we still think it is a useful way to think about options for the future of work. Let's take a closer look at the word *hybrid*.

Kevin has long served on the board of directors of Ag Alumni Seed, one of the world's largest providers of hybrid popcorn seed in the world. Here's how hybrid popcorn is created.

Two different varieties are carefully cross-pollenated to create a new hybrid plant. The breeders know that the new plant will be different than the parents. Each season, they create hundreds of new hybrid plants—all different from the originals. But that is just a small part of the story.

Although they know it will be *different*, they are aiming for *better*. To identify the new traits to be developed, they study, measure, and evaluate each plant based on the criteria they are breeding for. From hundreds of new plants, a few will be deemed better, to be tested again, and eventually these will be expanded to be a part of the product slate as new hybrids.

Importantly, we don't do all this work to produce one hybrid; as of this writing, the company sells twenty-four varieties of hybrid seed corn around the world. Why? Because the company sells different types of popcorn for different purposes, for different soil types, for variable growing conditions, and more.

Several lessons in this example have a direct application to the future paradigm of work.

- *Different isn't enough.* Whatever hybrid (whether it is working location, time of work, etc.) you try will be different than what you did in the past. Different isn't the bar, though; the goal is to create better. This means you might need to experiment and try different things before you find the different that is better for your team and organization.

- *Know what success is.* You can't determine better until you know what you are solving for. That is why the questions in the previous section are so important—and why you must keep Outcomes/Others properly balanced.

- *There is more than one right answer.* This book provides you guidance to find the "hybrid" that works best with your goals and environment. Slapping a generic model or plan into your situation might be a place to start, but it won't ultimately get you the best results.

Making New Better

The world of work in the postindustrial, post-Covid age will be different. The challenge we all face isn't about being different, but about crafting what will be better for our situation. You will only get to your version of better when you learn the lessons of the past, bring the hearts and minds of your team together, and apply the ideas in this book. As you do that, you'll create what work means for you—and you'll write a little history at the same time.

Final Thoughts

You knew work was changing when you picked up this book. Hopefully this chapter gives you more context and helps you think about this in new and important ways and with additional perspective. You'll need that as you read and apply the ideas in the rest of the book.

Chapter 5

The 3C Model for Team and Culture Design

For several months, Julio has been asking many of the questions we are posing in this book. He has been asking himself questions like "What are the components I need to consider when thinking about how to design teams in this new world of work?" and "How will I know if we succeeded?" As he thinks about creating an aspirational culture, he doesn't know what should be included. His hesitance in moving forward on these critical issues is due, in part, to these important questions. He knows he needs to do something, but he doesn't know where to start.

We wrote this book for people like Julio. We know the issues of team design and culture have always been important. But everyone is caught up in a time of rapid change in the workplace. We are looking at new ways and means of working, and the key factors that lead to successful teams and great cultures need to be spelled out and made simple and clear.

In *The Long-Distance Leader*, we introduced the Three O Model of Leadership, and in *The Long-Distance Teammate* we introduced the 3P

Model of Remote-Work Success. As we developed those models, and more importantly, as we have refined and used them with clients, we have found the power in the simplicity and the richness of their use.

One thing that has developed since March of 2020 when the Covid pandemic struck most companies in the US and Europe is the increased adoption of *hybrid teams*. Although the term gets thrown around a lot, it's often used as a catch-all for any team that isn't wholly remote or completely co-located.

The more we learn about this way of working, the more we realize that if our teams are to be truly hybrid going forward, they need to be very different from the teams we would design if we were just trying to re-create the office environment. We already know that following that old template leads to too many meetings, email overload, and a lack of flexibility around when people are working. If you are designing for a hybrid team, think of it as designing something unique and taking the opportunity to really change how you and your team works.

The goal is to create an equally useful and usable model to help you design, or redesign, your team for long-distance work. As with the other models, we believe the power of the 3C Model lies in simplicity. This model will help you design your team and your culture. Before we get ahead of ourselves though, let's describe what it is.

The 3C Model for Team and Culture Design

The 3C Model consists of three factors, and its power comes from integrating them and recognizing that they are interdependent on each other. The 3Cs are

- Communication
- Collaboration
- Cohesion

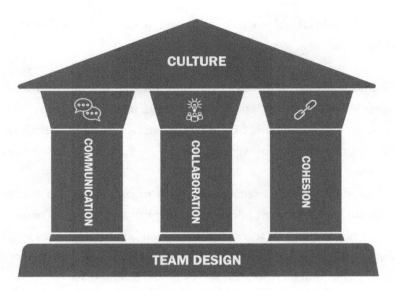

Figure 2: The 3C Model. Copyright Kevin Eikenberry Group.

Not only do all these components start with the same letter (making them easier to remember), but these words are also familiar. To understand the power of this model (see Figure 2), we need to define and describe these terms in the context of team and culture design.

Communication

Communicating is fundamental to being human—we have been communicating our entire lives. It is also a foundation of work. Although we all communicate, the skill, accuracy, and effectiveness of that communication varies widely. Communication is successful when messages are sent, received as intended, and mutually understood. In short, *message sent, message received, message understood.*

Everyone's work requires communication, and all work will be more successful when communication outcomes are more effective and achieved more rapidly. In an interconnected and interdependent world, even the individual craftsman needs to communicate with customers and suppliers.

Therefore, communication is critical and foundational to all work, and no matter how long we have been doing it or how well we do it, we can improve. When everyone was in the same building or location, we could have direct, immediate, rich, face-to-face conversations. As the barriers and challenges to great communication have grown, our need for it to be more effective has grown too.

One of our favorite examples of how hard communication is comes from a study of communication in operating rooms.[*] Trained observers watched ninety hours of team communication across forty-eight surgical procedures. Nearly one third of all the communications observed were classified as "communication failures" using this framework:

- **Timing:** Was the communication delivered at the best or needed time?

- **Content:** Was the information complete and accurate?

- **Audience:** Are the right people hearing and receiving the messages?

- **Purpose:** Are issues properly resolved?

Further, the study found that 36.4 percent of the failures resulted in inefficiency, team tension, resource waste, delays, inconvenience for the patient, and procedural errors.

This leaves us with two conclusions: If communication can fail or be suboptimal when people are side by side in real time during important

---

[*] L. Lingard, S. Espin, S. Whyte, G. Regehr, G. R. Baker, R. Reznick, J. Bohnen, B Orser, D. Doran, and E. Grober, "Communication Failures in the Operating Room: An Observational Classification of Recurrent Types and Effects," *Quality and Safety in Health Care* 13, no. 5 (October 2004): 330–34, https://doi.org/10.1136/qhc.13.5.330.

work, we know that when we add distance and other barriers, it will be even more challenging. And second, look at the results of the communication errors—you don't have to work in an operating room to recognize these failures as having potentially disastrous outcomes.

Communication must be effective in every part of your organizational activities and across all these groups/individuals:

- Within the team

- Between individuals on the team

- Across teams

- Between peers

- With leaders

- With customers and suppliers (internal and external)

When communication is poor, late, incomplete, or completely lacking, you get

- Misunderstanding

- Conflict

- Lack of alignment

- Poor leadership

- Missed opportunities

- Poor relationships

- Reduced trust

- Reduced commitment and engagement

- Reduced accountability

- Reduced speed in delivery of work

- Slow or ineffective change

- Reduced collaboration

- Increased frustration

- Increased turnover

- \<Add from your own experiences.>

When we look at it this way, it is easy to see why, even in the best and most successful organizations, we hear the following statement: "We need better communication." Communication has always been hard, but in a new world of work that is increasingly complex and done at distance, it is more critical than ever.

Collaboration

Merriam-Webster defines *collaborate* as

> *To work jointly with others or together especially in an intellectual endeavor.*

What *jointly* and *together* meant seemed much clearer when everyone worked with each other in the same building. When Gina needed to collaborate with George, she stopped by his office or cubicle and asked if he had a few minutes. Often the collaboration happened immediately. When Juan wanted some input on a problem, he might gather three or four people (or call a quick meeting in the conference room) to create that moment of collaboration. When the people you want to collaborate with are in other parts of town, the country, or the globe, it doesn't seem as easy.

For so long, collaboration was viewed in terms of

- Real-time interaction

- A conference room

- A whiteboard or flip chart

- PowerPoint slides or other sharing of data

Although all these things can be replicated in a virtual setting, most people have found that collaboration is harder virtually than face to face. There is no doubt that there are advantages to face-to-face collaboration (our long-standing virtual team looks forward to our infrequent in-person meetings). However, meeting distantly can have positive, often unexpected, advantages.

There are at least three flaws in the "we have to be in person to collaborate" mindset:

- *Collaboration isn't just an event.* Collaboration can exist without and beyond a meeting. There is something about the energy that can come from an in-person meeting, but we have both also spent decades hearing from people about how ineffective meetings are. If you think about collaboration as taking place only at formal (or even informal) meetings, you aren't thinking about this subject as broadly as you could or should be.

- *Collaboration isn't just a synchronous activity.* Back to the definition: we know that working "jointly" doesn't have to mean at the same time. Email, for all its challenges and shortcomings, has provided all of us with plenty of positive collaboration examples. There are plenty of other newer collaboration tools—including those that replace and enhance the venerable whiteboard—that can create fantastic collaboration results. How often have you left a meeting and thought of a follow-up question or an additional idea and been disappointed because the meeting is over and it's too late? Ongoing discussion threads in Microsoft Teams or Slack can improve the quality of decision-making or creative problem solving.

- *Face-to-face collaboration won't always be possible.* If part of the team is in Bangor, and the rest is in Bangalore, you will likely never be in the same room (or even in the same time zone). You will have to learn to make the best of the situation.

Plenty of factors play into collaboration success. All these need to be considered as you design your teams and culture.

- Meetings/huddles and gatherings

- One-on-one collaborations

- Brainstorming

- Problem solving

- Planning

- Creating a common vision and purpose

When you look at this list separate from the word *collaboration*, you can see that all these things have been and can be done effectively at a distance when we institute plans, processes, and agreements to support that success. It is important to note that we are not saying we shouldn't or can't gather. What we are saying is that if we think about collaboration in a staid and conservative way, we may miss the chance to have great collaboration when we have a distance and asynchronous component in our team design.

Cohesion

The third part of the 3C Model is cohesion. Here is the first definition from *Merriam-Webster*:

The act or state of sticking together tightly

Is it paradoxical to stick together tightly if we never (or rarely) work in physical proximity? Perhaps if you think literally, but let's not stop there.

The second definition ties the word to biology and the life sciences:

The union between similar plant parts or organs

We like the biology connection and connotation of the word, and it's why we chose it. Work and working relationships aren't solely mechanical or defined by org charts, time, and space. Cohesion implies something beyond those things. The Cohesion dimension includes decidedly nonstructural things like these:

- Relationships

- Connection

- Relatedness

- Trust

- Belief

- Purpose

- Meaning

- Engagement

- Inclusion

- Accountability

Each of these dimensions is critical to team success.

Again, our experience may cloud our judgement here—we may think about how these things may be easier to create or sustain when we are in-person. Although that point can be made, look at any one of these items and you can also make a case for doing them at a distance.

Ask these questions:

- Can we create relationships in a flexible working situation?

- Can people be engaged in a remote or hybrid working environment?

- Can accountability be supported when people rarely see each other?

Yes, yes, and yes.

Traditionally most of the items on this list have been treated as either skills (therefore a training/coaching issue) or hopes ("We hope we get these" or "We see these in our best performers") rather than as expectations and design elements of our teams. We encourage you to, and will show you in the rest of the book how to, make each of these considerations in your team design and culture, rather than letting them remain hopes and wishes.

How to Use the 3C Model

You can use this framework both for team design and culture creation. We will help you do both. Inside of those two purposes, you can use the 3C Model to do three things:

- *Assess.* Examine each of the dimensions (individually or collectively) to determine how a team is doing currently in that area (more on this in the next section).

- *Design.* Use these dimensions to help us create a complete and clear team design so that our team can deliver on each dimension successfully. We can use each dimension to clarify our aspirational culture as well.

- *Develop.* It is one thing to design or decide what we want. It is another entirely to be able to get there. The 3C Model can point us to what we need to develop toward our team and culture goals.

The Questions That Further Define the Dimensions

Although we are writing about designing teams for a new world of work and intentionally creating a culture, we know that most people aren't starting from scratch. If you're reading with an existing team you are likely thinking: How are we doing now?

Whether now or later—really at any time—you can use the 3C Model as an assessment tool to gauge your current state.

Use the following questions as an individual mental exercise, or use them more valuably and reliably in conversations with your team(s) or in a survey format. Even if you decide to do an individual assessment first, we encourage you to use questions like these with your team.

COMMUNICATION QUESTIONS

- What is our frustration level with team communication?

- How often do miscommunications cause conflict or rework?

- How clearly are the team goals communicated from the perspective of those receiving those messages?

- How effectively do we communicate across the team and throughout the organization?

- How frequently does the full team communicate in formal and informal ways?

- How successfully do team members communicate—both synchronously and asynchronously?

- How often do we default to communication tools and practices that are most comfortable, rather than those that are the most effective?

- How well do parties share the responsibility for communication (between sender and receiver)?

- What can we do to improve team communication today?

- On a scale of 1 to 10, how do all team members rate the communication success of the team?

COLLABORATION QUESTIONS

- How effective are our meetings at reaching the desired outcomes and needs of the work?

- Do our meetings maintain/improve trust and relationships, or hurt them?

- How well do we use asynchronous collaboration tools?

- How often and successfully do we collaborate informally?

- What does our collaboration look like across teams?

- How much does hierarchy or reporting relationships get in the way of our collaboration?

- How much collaboration takes place in our planning processes?

- Do people feel heard and feel that their ideas are considered?

- How often are projects done on time and on budget?

- On a scale of 1 to 10, how do all team members rate the collaboration on our team?

COHESION QUESTIONS

- How much psychological safety exists on our team? Would everyone rate this in the same way?

- What is the overall level of trust across our team?

- How strong are the working relationships on our team?

- How connected and aligned do people feel with their leader/ manager?

- How aligned are we to the mission and purpose of our work?

- How would we rate the overall level of engagement on the team?

- How much accountability do people feel and exhibit toward team outcomes?

- How clear are the expectations across the team?

- On a scale of 1 to 10, how do all team members rate our team cohesion?

If you choose to work through these questions as a team, you might want to get a facilitator from outside of the team so that all team members can contribute effectively. In our experience much good will come from these conversations, even if the team determines they have a long way to go—that they need to improve communication, enhance collaboration, and build trust using the conversation itself.

Final Thoughts

The 3C Model is comprehensive yet simple. It is meant to be used by leaders, teams, and individuals—all with the goal of helping you create and advance your teams in a world that may include people working at distance from each other part or all the time.

The visual of the model (Figure 2) implies an important point—having just one pillar in good shape isn't enough. To have a solid foundation and a sturdy roof, we need strength in all three areas. To be sure, getting this right in person isn't easy and it can be harder to do at distance, but it can be done. This model helps us get from possible to success. The rest of the book will help you use this model in all your team designs and redesigns as well as with your macro- and microcultural design pursuits.

Part III

Designing for Success

A new working situation requires a new look at how we design teams. In the next two chapters we will provide you with a process for designing teams collaboratively whether you are starting from scratch or re-designing an existing team for these new realities.

Chapter 6

Designing Your Team

Rajesh believes teams can be designed differently. He doesn't think the cookie-cutter approach or even the existing structure needs to be followed—especially in a long-distance working world. He isn't in HR or Organizational Development; he is a line manager who wants teams to be more effective—especially when the team is hybrid. He feels he should have a process to help him think about the relevant issues and bring his team along with him so that together they can design a team to which everyone can commit to get better results.

There is a way to do what Rajesh wants to achieve, and in this chapter, we are going to lay out the process. Here are the high-level steps:

1. Think big picture—create your dream design.

2. Apply the design considerations.

3. Finalize a team design based on your situation.

We are talking about the structure of the team. What work does our team need to do? What roles and tasks are required? What is the best order in which to do those tasks? How can we create greater efficiency and effectiveness? It's the structure of the team that we are focusing on here. *How* work will get done is a culture question. That question is equally important, but we will examine it separately in coming chapters.

You might wonder, Is the process different for a new team versus an existing one? Although you should consider some differences (and we'll help you with them), the overall *process* is the same. The questions you ask, and the way you identify the most critical components of the design, will be the key to a successful process and having the kinds of conversations that create a finished product everyone can buy into. This thoughtful approach will also be the first giant step to building a culture team members will thrive in going forward.

Commitment versus Compliance

For any team design to be successful, the people involved must be *committed* to both the long-term aims of the team and the day-to-day work. Some call this commitment *buy-in*. While buy-in is nice, commitment is a much stronger state. Commitment is internally driven. When we choose to become emotionally invested in something, we put more thought, effort, and passion into it. We anticipate challenges and find creative ways to address them. We simply try harder when we have a mental and emotional stake in the success of that work.

The alternative is compliance. *Compliance* is when someone follows the rules and meets (often barely) expectations. It is meant to achieve standards set by an outside entity, often your boss or the organization. When we comply, we often put out just enough effort to achieve the goal. Sometimes, it's done grudgingly. We've all seen incidents of "grudging compliance," where people technically meet the expectation, but don't put in the slightest effort or proactivity. "Hey, you said you wanted it by Friday, you didn't tell me it had to be good."

You've experienced both states yourself. As a youngster, if your mother told you to clean your room or you couldn't go out, you did a lot of grousing and complaining, and probably experienced some conflict with her. She might have had to inspect your work several times until the room met her standards. (Why did she always look under the bed?) Eventually you passed her standards and were free to go. On the other hand, if you had friends coming over, or if you just decided to take it upon yourself to clean your room, you almost always completed the task more cheerfully and better (even under the bed).

What makes the difference? Human beings are more powerfully motivated from within than externally. This is an important factor to keep in mind when designing your team. Is this new entity something that's been dictated to them, and that they must comply with? Or are they involved from the beginning, excited about it, and committed to its success? Obviously the committed team is better. To commit to the design, people must feel they have contributed to creating it and their ideas and concerns have been heard and considered.

As the leader, it's easy to think it's your job to bring a plan to the team. You've probably been thinking about it longer, and it feels more efficient to bring them something that's already started. But be aware that this approach can easily backfire. Remember that communication, collaboration, and cohesion cannot be mandated. Additionally, the collective work on the design can strengthen the three pillars of the model in real time during real conversations.

Think about your leader bringing a design for the team to you and your teammates. Maybe you didn't even know this discussion was coming. Maybe you agreed that a new design could help, but you haven't had time to think about it. Now, the leader lays out the "draft" for you and asks for your feedback and commitment.

At best, a draft will narrow the frame of the conversation to your leader's perspective—which might already be limiting. At worst it will leave the team feeling that the boss has already decided and any significant conversation is futile. If, as a leader, you *have* already decided, don't ask the team for their input, and don't expect anything more than weak compliance either.

The ultimate success of the design depends on the team's commitment to it as much as it does to the design itself. And importantly, the way you do this work sets cultural precedents. If you bring a "draft," you are telling people that their job is to approve what leadership shares. We hope that isn't your intent. In other words, how you create and finalize your design is almost as important as the design itself.

So how do you avoid the pitfalls and improve the chances that you gain commitment?

Co-creating Your Dream Design

We suggest you start this exercise by bringing the team together with a blank sheet of paper and an optimistic mindset. Yes, there may be realities and constraints to consider, but if you start by imposing them, the team may "settle" too quickly or not realize that more is possible than initially thought.

What you're trying to do is create a vision of a team designed to handle all the components you have to consider:

- The purpose of the work

- The nature of the work

- The roles required

- The location and time in which the work is done

- The tools and processes

- The needed skills and knowledge

Plus, the 3C considerations:

- Communication

- Collaboration

- Cohesion

Each team member should consider all these factors as they ask themselves, What would be the ideal design for our team?

The Design Questions

Your goal is to get everyone thinking about this for themselves, then bring the team together so the outcome is more than the sum of the parts. You should consider several questions to get to a picture of your dream design. Task each team member with thinking about each of these questions and capturing their notes and ideas. Remind everyone to think without constraints or assumptions and not to be overly influenced by the current state.

It's tempting for us to show you an example, but every organization's and team's needs vary widely, and we don't want to influence you too early in the process. A customer service call center incented by response time will have very different answers for their design than a coding team whose job is to turn out bug-free software. As we mentioned before, there will be tradeoffs. The following questions will help you identify and prioritize what's important and unique to your team and needs.

The purpose of the work. Think bigger than the tasks.

- Why do we do this work and who do we do it for?

- What do they expect and need?

- How do these answers factor into the team design?

The nature of the work. Think about the needed work and desired work, not simply the current work. You are thinking about what you want and need, not reordering the deck chairs.

- What is the work of this team?

- What is delivered to whom?

- Who are the customers?

- How and when must we communicate to/with them?

- Is the work project based, or process based?

- How is the final work product affected by communication?

- Does the work require inputs from multiple sources?

- How do these answers factor into the team design?

The roles required. For an existing team, as hard as it will be, don't think people or names yet. Think roles.

- What roles are required?

- What skills are needed to complete the required work?

- How many people are needed?

- How do these answers factor into the design?

The location and the time in which the work is done. Think about what the work requires first—you will get to your personal desires and real-world constraints later.

- Which tasks can be done in isolation or alone?

- How much flexibility in terms of location and time does the work allow?

- Which tasks require collaboration?

- Does that collaboration need to be in person?

- Does the work require frequent, fast answers to questions?

- How do these answers factor into the design?

The tools and processes. Here you might look at what exists to help you see the gaps and overlaps.

- What is needed to accomplish what you have identified?

- What systems and tools will help?

- What is in the way?

- What is still needed?

- How do these answers factor into the design?

The needed skills and knowledge. Think about selection, onboarding, training, and development of team members, including new hires.

- What experience do people need to bring to, or develop on, the team?

- How much industry or professional experience is needed?

- What perspectives or mindsets are required?

- What do people need to be able to know and do to accomplish the work effectively and efficiently?

- What technical or role-specific skills are needed on the team?

- What role would mentoring need to play?

How do these answers factor into the design? Beyond these questions about the work and context of it, consider questions relating to the 3Cs as well.

Communication in our dream design.

- What processes and tools will reduce conflict and misunderstanding?

- What types of messages need to be shared in what ways?

- How important is synchronous communication to completing the work?

- How much cross-team and cross-department communication is needed/desired?

Collaboration in our dream design.

- What level of interdependent work is required/desired?

- What is the role of meetings to deliver the work product?

- What role does brainstorm and problem solving play in completing this work?

- How will decisions be made?

Cohesion in our dream design.

- How important are relationships between team members to our success?

- How important is trust to the team's work? How do we design that in?

- What level of engagement is required? How do we design that in?

- How important is diversity of thought, opinion, experience, perspective, and background in successfully completing this work?

We know there are a lot of questions. Some will generate very detailed thinking; others may not apply to your team, or the answers may be simple. Every team member may not write a paragraph, or even three bullet points, on each one. Depending on each member's job, some of these questions will be more important or personal to them than others. But everyone needs to think about the range and scope of these questions so they can start to create their personal picture of the ideally designed team.

Go to LongDistanceTeamBook.com/Questions to download a pdf of these questions and a brief introduction and instructions to share with your team.

What Will These Initial Designs Look Like?

There isn't a one-size-fits-all answer here. The objective is for everyone to have ideas about what the ideal team design would look like that are clear to them and that they can share with others. You may want to include bullet points in response to some/all of these questions, examples, pictures, diagrams, maybe even an org chart (though we are talking about something far richer than that here) at this information-gathering and daydreaming stage.

How to Make the Process a Success

It would be lovely if we could just go to the team members and ask them what the perfect team design should be and have everyone's answer be the same. You know that won't be the case, however, and the richness of different opinions and perspectives will give you a better result, even if it might cause temporary conflict or disagreement.

When engaging the team, the leader must lead without being "the boss." In fact, you probably want someone outside of the team to facilitate the conversation. A skilled outside person can help the team openly share and stay on task and can give them team the opportunity for candid, plentiful input without judgment.

There are four things that must be included in these conversations as you create your collective design.

- *Clear expectations for the process and outcome.* Everyone needs to know what the intended outcome of this work will be.

- *Psychological safety.* This is defined as "being able to show and employ oneself without fear of negative consequences of self-image, status or career."[*] People need to know it is safe for them to share their ideas, and they need to be open to the ideas of others, too. Not that you should be concerned about people actually attacking each other (unless your team needs a full-scale intervention), but being close to each other is often fraught with potential negative energy. Will people be comfortable critiquing an idea when the person who made it is sitting right next to them? Will they raise that controversial issue when the boss is giving them a dirty look from across the

---

[*] William A. Kahn, "Psychological Conditions of Personal Engagement and Disengagement at Work," *Academy of Management Journal* 33, no. 4 (December 1990): 692–724. https://www.jstor.org/stable/256287.

table? Can they point out the obvious flaw in Bob's idea when they have to go back to their cubicle and sit next to Bob? Will people be comfortable sharing their ideas with people they have rarely seen or have never met?

- *Equitable airtime.* Help people believe that their ideas will be heard and fairly evaluated. If the conversation is taking place as a hybrid meeting, pay special attention to getting the input and ideas from those attending at a distance.

- *A great answer, not necessarily your personal choice.* Remind people that, likely, no one will be happy with every part of the final result, but that most will see their fingerprints on the design enough to commit to, not merely comply with, the result.

More on Psychological Safety

If you're trying to do your best to be a fair and supportive leader, it can feel a bit off-putting to think your people don't feel safe. You aren't vindictive. You welcome fresh and even contradictory ideas. You're a good person. Right?

It doesn't really matter.

There is a built-in power differential on every team.

Think of it this way. When your manager says to you, "We need to talk," what's your initial reaction? Even if you have a great relationship, you probably spend a moment wondering what you did wrong or preparing yourself for bad news.

On teams, the manager's reaction isn't the only reason people may fear for their psychological safety. If they question a teammate's suggestion, will it cause tension? Will that other person seek payback? If your team prides itself on its collegiality and everyone getting along, will team members speak up and raise uncomfortable issues? Will anyone listen if they do speak?

The foundation of psychological safety is trust. Do people trust that the organization really wants and values their input? Do they trust they can give their manager feedback that won't be held against them? Do they trust their teammates will take input as intended and not take it personally?

As we've mentioned in *The Long-Distance Leader* and *The Long-Distance Teammate* there are three components to trust on a team:

- **Common Purpose:** Is everyone aligned around what the work is and why we're here?

- **Competence:** Talk is cheap. Can everyone demonstrate they are competent to do the job expected of them at an acceptable level?

- **Motivation:** Are people motivated to do the best they can? Are they honest? Do they have the team's best interest at heart? Are they (or will they be) good teammates?

Now you're ready to engage the team in this exciting process. Take the next steps with an eye to getting the best, most honest input possible, and do all you can to create a psychologically safe environment where trust is as high as possible.

All these factors—the power differential, psychological safety, and trust—are reasons we suggest having someone other than the leader facilitate these discussions.

Regardless of who facilitates, if the meeting is synchronous (whether in person, hybrid, or totally virtual) make sure you consider these guidelines:

- *Set expectations for getting everyone's input in a safe environment.* Make time and space for everyone. Let people know that if someone calls on them, it is because their input is desired, and that it is okay to say, "I don't have anything to add," if they don't.

- *Don't allow interruptions.* This is important. People may feel strongly about something a teammate says or feel the need to defend their idea. When someone is offering input, allow interruptions only to answer relevant questions or to clarify the idea. Otherwise, the team should listen respectfully. They'll all get their turn.

- *Create space for everyone.* Some individuals may tend to dominate the discussion. If you tell everyone they will be heard, live up to that promise. It may mean exercising patience coaxing answers out of people, but it is important!

- *If your team is large, consider breakout groups.* This allows people who might be intimidated or shy about sharing ideas in a larger group to feel more comfortable and included. Small groups are also a great way to help control any negative power dynamics. You can use breakout rooms in both in-person and virtual meetings. For example, if Terri is Bob's manager, he may be more willing to speak up in a group where she isn't shooting him daggers across the table or over the webcam.

Before You Bring Everyone to the Office

We often use workplace language that was applicable in the past but less so now. We still "hang up" a phone, even though the equipment no longer hangs on a wall. When we talk about "bringing people together," it's easy to default to physical meetings. In today's distributed workplace, that is neither practical, nor particularly desirable.

Time zones. Dispersed teams. Unavailability of conference rooms. There are plenty of reasons to think of asynchronous events as second best or making the best of a bad situation.

In fact, leveraging technology and using time and distance effectively can often improve the quality of your inputs and help you reach better decisions—including in these team design sessions.

Over the last few years, research has shown that virtual meetings sometimes generate more honest feedback than meeting in person, especially from women and less senior members of the team. Not having to withstand dirty looks or shout louder than the office blowhard in order to be heard can make for more equitable and robust discussions.

Physical distance is one of the factors. And although bringing everyone's thinking together could well mean a meeting(s), not all the work has to be done by getting together at the same time. The process to gain input and agreement on the team design requires gathering information, encouraging input, reaching decisions, and communicating those to the world.

Yes, email is helpful. But tools like Slack, Microsoft Teams, and specific project management software like Monday.com or Trello* can be very helpful. Using Microsoft Visio or similar tools for laying out flowcharts or organization charts might help people visualize how the team will be structured and assist their thinking.

Taking time to analyze options and craft thoughtful responses is often easier when people have time to think. They aren't assessing an idea in real time with everyone staring at them, waiting for an answer.

Giving people something written to work with will help those with different first languages than the one you are working in. The speed at which some people speak in meetings can be both intimidating and confusing, leading some to hesitate or not participate. As teams become more culturally and nationally diverse, times when you can level the playing field will work to the team's advantage.

In addition, asynchronous tools allow for anonymous feedback. Slack and Teams have the option to create specific topic discussion rooms with the ability to turn off participants' names. If that isn't practical, have the

---

* Technology changes quickly. At this writing, these are the most common tools used, but in the future they might (probably will) be replaced by something else. The point is to look at, and maximize, what's available to you. The specific name of the tool is less important than how you use what you have at your disposal.

feedback go to someone whose job is to create a document with all the ideas, with the names removed.

And when calendars, time zones, and other work keep us from getting a meeting scheduled, it doesn't mean we can't get started. As an example, Kevin often records meetings so that people who can't make the meeting have access to the information shared and know what was discussed. People are expected to view those recordings when they can, and he follows up with one-on-one conversations to confirm that the information was received and to answer any questions.

If someone can't be there, they can get up to speed and then share their questions and comments in another asynchronous way or in a conversation with the leader. Recordings also allow for transcriptions that might be helpful in your ongoing conversations (or for nonnative speakers) as well.

When You Bring Everyone Together

Time zones and logistics permitting, it's a good idea to kick off the process with a full team meeting (in person or via your online meeting platform). This will not only be the richest way to communicate your own enthusiasm and the importance of the project, but it will give the team a chance to ask questions, and express their own ideas, concerns, and excitement about the project. This also allows everyone to be on the same page, at the same time.

Be clear about how you'll gather, process, and share the information. This process will feel like a form of brainstorming. Plenty of books and resources cover brainstorming techniques, but you're at a point where you are still gathering ideas and building trust that people will be heard. Whether you are all in-person or meeting online, here are some important things to remember:

■ Write down all ideas and suggestions exactly as stated with as little judgment as possible.

- Clarify ideas before writing them down so you aren't unwittingly editing suggestions or sending signals about an item's acceptability.

- Don't always lean on volunteers to go first. Often those most eager to share their ideas have outsized influence with the team or might create an environment where contrary ideas get shut down.

- Try to alternate between senior and newer members of the team. Many people are reluctant to speak up early, and by the time their turn comes, the usual people have all had their say and new ideas may get lost.

- Leverage the diversity of the team in these design sessions. Avoid behaviors and systems that exclude people (often unintentionally). Make a point of getting input early from those who might have unique perspectives. This is modelling the type of equity and inclusion you surely want on your team.

- Using webcams is valuable. If online, people should be on camera when they are speaking. There are plenty of reasons not to have folks stare into a webcam for hours at a time, but when they are speaking and answering questions about their ideas, rich communication is important.

- Getting agreement is important. Find ways to vote that don't expose people to their peers. A great way to do that is weighted voting, where people get to choose their first option but also express a second or third choice.

This isn't to suggest that all team interaction (for these design conversations and in general) should be all synchronous or all offline. In fact, a blended approach is often best. Imagine the results if you had a meeting to outline the plan, introduce the process, and answer questions or concerns. Then people had time on their own or in small groups to think about their answers to the team design questions. A first cut of ideas and suggestions might be done asynchronously before having a live meeting to discuss answers, build on suggestions, and weed out irrelevant information or information not worth considering further. Then people can go off to noodle some more, without the pressure of time and impatient peers, and then submit further information and ideas.

Voting and decision making can be done synchronously or asynchronously, but you will want to document all decisions and perhaps meet for the purpose of explaining the final decisions, clarifying any questions or misunderstandings, and generating enthusiasm for your team's final design.

Finally, set timeframes for the input. Give people enough time to be thoughtful, yet make sure you still create urgency and clear deadlines for participation. As the leader, you'll want to build in check-ins and reminders to make sure people participate and take advantage of the opportunity to be part of the process.

It would be lovely to think that the meeting will be so successful and inspirational that you can coalesce on a design in one meeting and people will be able to leave and get started right away. For all kinds of reasons that's unlikely. People need time to ponder each other's input and think about these responses. Likely the team will need to make (hopefully small) tweaks based on this work. It's a good idea to have the entire process (including the reasons behind the project) documented and placed somewhere it can be easily accessed. A shared drive, a SharePoint site, or dedicated discussion rooms in Teams or Slack will likely be very helpful.

Documenting the Final Design and Gaining Commitment

Everyone has thought about it and shared their ideas and you've documented your dream design. You're almost there.

Almost.

Planning is only as effective as the execution. While the Prussian General Carl von Clausewitz said, "everyone has a battle plan until the first cannon shot," and Mike Tyson famously said, "everyone has a fight plan until they get punched in the mouth," they knew what they were talking about. For a plan to be executed, people must understand it and commit to it.

Several steps are required to document this plan. You're not just creating a wish list and an archive of how you and the team have been spending your time. You need proper documentation to allow for mapping against any constraints that exist (more on this in the next chapter), and so the team can continuously monitor and improve its performance. Such documentation helps the leader coach team members more effectively and maintain the commitment of individual teammates.

What should be documented, and how should it be handled?

- Keep your original notes and any completed documents where anyone can easily access and refer to them.

- Keep your implementation plans in the same location.

These documents should be used to set performance expectations. They are vital tools for coaching and maintaining the team's journey to excellence.

Once goals and expectations are set for each role, individuals should be able to map their work to that of the team. Understanding where they fit into the overall design provides them with a big picture that can enhance their commitment to their teammates and the outcomes. Coaching is easier when the goals and expected behaviors have been clear and transparent from the beginning. When a record of the team design exists, it's simple to help people be accountable. "I didn't know," isn't really a viable excuse.

Once the team is up and running, the plan continues to be important. When decisions need to be made, the team should refer to the original plan.

Does this new situation impact the plan? How should our response fit the goals we've set?

One thing Kevin has done for years is use the team's agreed-upon guidelines to frame discussions during meetings. For example, the Kevin Eikenberry Group has very clear Mission, Vision, and Values statements. Most team meetings contain a quick reminder of those and how all decisions made must fit those criteria.

If you find it useful, here's what those look like:

Mission   Making a REMARKABLE difference . . . for leaders and future leaders, their teams, their organizations, and the world.

Vision   Recognized as a global leadership thought leader, The Kevin Eikenberry Group creates and promotes powerful learning tools and experiences. Through our efforts and partnerships, we help organizations and leaders change the world for the better every day.

Values   Authenticity, Balance, Learning and Growth, Leadership, Relationships, Meaningful Work, Inspiration

You should share the final design plan with the team, both synchronously and asynchronously. Make sure to share it somewhere people can access and refer to it, no matter the time zone or time of day. Sharing the result live, with as many people as possible, will help you build commitment.

Remember that although people choose to engage or not, it's usually not a simple, personal decision. People choose to commit to things that matter to them personally but also fit a social need. If you saw your teammates committing to a vision and promising to uphold their ends of the bargain, wouldn't you be more likely to as well?

When you've been part of the design process, when you've been heard and had your input valued, there's a greater chance you'll commit to the team's long-term success.

If you're an individual, you have more reasons to be engaged. The solution is not a mandate from "on high," but one you've contributed to. You have an emotional, psychological, and social stake in the team's success and a clear vision of what great work looks like.

If you're a team leader, the team design allows for more effective coaching, performance management, and process improvement, leading to sustained success.

If you're a senior leader, your people have helped you create a team design. It will be your responsibility to help put structures and processes in place that achieve those ambitious goals.

Final Thoughts

It's been a long, complex process to design a team that will get the work done and help everyone, from the individual team member to the CEO, succeed. Remember that how the plan is executed, and how people interact within its structures, will determine if your organization is a place people want to work. In our experience, achieving this will be work, but if you apply what you have learned here, people will be energized by the result, and chances are, all three Cs in the 3C Model will be strengthened during the process.

Chapter 7

Redesigning an Existing Team

Alice's last team was extremely successful, and everyone raved about their positive, energetic culture and the way everyone worked together to achieve the team's goals. She's been promoted to a new division, and her new assignment is a challenge. The team she's inherited is mostly made up of long-time employees. For reasons she can't discern, they have a reputation for being stubborn and not cooperating with other divisions or parts of the company. Additionally, their last manager left, frustrated, because not only did it seem that most of the team refused to buy into the company-assigned goals, but they also consistently missed targets. Alice is clear on what her ideal team looks like; it seems very different from the reality she's walked into.

In the last chapter, we looked at designing a team and laying the groundwork for creating the team you want when *you're starting from scratch.* But most of us will be in a different situation, one similar to Alice's. Like Alice, you may find yourself faced with an already established team. As the old saying goes, "you need to fix the boat while it's in the water."

The difference between conjuring up the team you envision from scratch and redesigning and changing how an existing team functions is not "yes, but"; instead it's "yes, and." *Yes,* all the design factors that go into building a team apply, whether the team already exists or not. *And,* there are several complicating factors. For example, the people who are already doing the work have a routine, and the fact that the where and when of the work is now changing may cause resistance.

Although you will include the team in this process, at this stage, you are probably trying to get your own thoughts in order. This means we need to add a step—the new step 3—to the process we've already shared. Now the steps look like this:

1. Think big picture—create your dream design.

2. Apply the design considerations.

3. *Look at the situation and constraints that you might not be able to talk about with the team.*

4. Finalize team design together.

After you have done your dreaming with the team, you need to look at the current situation. The team may be able to help you with some of this analysis, but some pieces may still fall to you as the leader. Before you finalize your design, consider the following:

- Who are the current team members?

- What does the existing team design and structure look like?

- What other constraints exist?

- How do the existing situation and design impact the 3Cs (Communication, Collaboration, and Cohesion)?

Who Are the Current Team Members?

The team has drafted a new design, but at some point, you're going to have to assign names to the roles. When the team exists, there's another wrinkle: there are already names assigned. Regardless of the size of the changes you are considering, you must look at the current players on the team.

- Who are your top performers?

- Who has the most experience?

- Who seems more committed to the changes being discussed?

- Who are the influencers and thought leaders?

- Who might fit best in any new roles or processes?

This is where reality sets in. We consciously wanted you to leave this thought process out of the initial steps because we didn't want you to—intentionally or not—design around specific people like Bob in Boise or Louise in London. When you begin to add names to job and role descriptions, you may find that one person will definitely resist change while someone in another role will champion the new process. Identifying possible barriers or champions will make planning implementation easier.

People are more than a job description; they are part of how the team works. In a perfect world, they're leaders and great teammates. Sometimes they are just average performers who don't exert any real influence on the team, positive or negative. They may propel the work forward productively or serve as obstacles. Dealing with these realities may impact your design, but don't adjust the design too much based on individuals. Recognize, instead, that you may need to provide additional coaching to help people adapt to the new design and the new approaches to make the whole thing work.

Ask yourself real-world questions like these:

- Do the current players allow us to get to our design or not?

- Can we get there with coaching and training, or do we have gaps that need to be filled in with new skills or information?

- Do our most experienced team members have the knowledge and skills to perform in the new ways the design suggests?

- Will Becca in Boston (or Bangalore) accept the changes or cause conflict?

- Will people's feelings about when and where they work be a help or hindrance to the changes?

- Will less experienced employees be ready to step up in new ways?

- How can we utilize our top performers to model the new desired behaviors and influence other team members?

Leaders must consider many of these questions alone or with a small group of counselors, not by sharing them in an instant message channel or email with the team. Such is the leader's responsibility. Thinking these questions through will help you improve how the team receives and implements your drafted design.

It is important to recognize that you shouldn't try to implement the design alone. Every team has members who influence others. Whether due to position, tenure, personality, relationships, or performance, these thought leaders/change agents are important to your implementation—especially when you're working with a Long-Distance Team. Make sure you help those thought leaders be influencers for positive, not lead the group to negative or cynical attitudes.

What Does the Existing Team Design and Structure Look Like?

Leaders need to think about the interpersonal dynamics at work. It's tempting to apply labels like, "team player" or "bad influence." Remember that these sorts of labels, whether positive or otherwise, are often biased and that might not be helpful.

What's needed is objective observation. Forget who people are, who they seem to be, or who they have been in the past; what's important is what they actually do. Remember that accurately assessing motives is impossible since whatever we think is often colored by our own feelings and attitudes. What matters is behavior—especially future behavior. Here are some examples of what we are talking about:

- What do people *do*? Which behaviors do the team members prioritize? What is rewarded both in performance reviews and in the social climate?

- What has happened/is happening in meetings that encourages the team to settle for slipshod work or choose to make quality decisions?

- What behaviors do the leaders engage in (positive or not) that influence the rest of the team?

- What do people in the rest of the organization do that supports or hinders your team's work? For example, if people receive tasks early but then just let them languish on someone's desk, it is obvious that time is not a priority to everyone.

- How do your answers to these questions impact the design you want to implement?

What Other Constraints Exist?

If your design determines that 85 percent of the work can be effectively done remotely, but the organization has determined that people will work in the office 50 percent of the time, you are faced with a disconnect. If your organization rewards *individual* effort through bonuses or other public recognition, but your design supports *team* success, how do you reconcile these two approaches?

Depending on where you sit in the organizational structure, you might be able to, or feel you aren't able to, affect big issues. If you are a middle manager in Paris or Peoria, for instance, you may not be able to do anything today, but don't give up hope. Although we don't live in your macroculture, if you are patient and persistent, you can still make change happen. In fact, the effort and quality of the work you have done in team design will be a powerful influence on the rest of the organization. It is possible that no one else will have put in the level of broad analysis of the work that you have. When you lay out your concerns or ask for exceptions, you might be surprised by the responses you receive.

Change starts small, and those small wins can create big successes. Is there any reason why you and your team can't start the snowball rolling?

If your design runs into roadblocks, be realistic, but not fatalistic. Share the work of your team upward and see what latitude you might have inside of existing policies and established norms to achieve your desired design. And if you can't get the changes or dispensations you need, share that with your team in an open way.

How Does the Existing Situation and Design Impact the 3Cs?

Your draft design considered your goals for the three pillars of communication, collaboration, and cohesion. What does the existing design look like in these areas? As you think through the current state, you might find big gaps in one or more of these areas. If you desire strong relationships in your design, but currently they are weak or nonexistent, you know you have work to do in in that area. If your meetings—whether in-person, virtual, or hybrid—are already relatively effective, you won't need to focus as much effort there. Consciously thinking about the differences between the current state and your future design in these three areas will help you prioritize where the team needs to spend the most time.

Finalize the Design

Once you have considered how your current reality will affect your design, you need to factor that into your final design. Even if you have to tweak, delay, or overhaul your draft, remember that the initial vision work was important. Don't lose that picture for you and the team. Perhaps you will just need to take an interim step before you can jump to your ultimate vision. Don't lose sight of your ultimate goal.

Come back to the team with your analysis and questions based on the work you have done in this chapter. You may be surprised by how on board they may be, and you will likely gain some valuable insight from them too. Continuing to engage them is the key to success in redesigning an existing team.

Final Thoughts

Implementing a design with a new group for new work is a big task that involves change, but refashioning a design and designing the boat while it's in the water requires a deeper level of change management/leadership skills. You have engaged people in a design for the future, but you must also take the current state into account. Remember that although existing habits, routines, and roles are hard to change, they can change.

Part IV

Creating Your Aspirational Culture

When a group gathers, a culture naturally develops. And the culture will change over time—especially if your work situation is changing. But will it change in the direction you want it to and support the organization, team, and results you want? Not necessarily. That's why we need to intentionally and collaboratively think about the type of culture we want—so that we can create it. In this set of chapters, you will learn about the tools and the processes you need to create cultures that will support your team and the results you want.

Chapter 8

Defining Your Aspirational Culture

Stephano is a CEO who feels like getting the culture right will be the missing piece to creating a high-performing organization. The organization is full of top talent, has a good mix of experience and energetic youth, and seems poised for great things. But something is missing. He is also concerned about the big changes that resulted from last year's merger. It feels like every team is different, and sometimes meeting (virtually or in person) with different groups feels like stepping into new countries or geographic regions. He really believes the culture is the key to unlocking greater success, but he just can't seem to find the lock.

The fictional Stephano reminds us of several C-suite executives we've worked with. They know culture is important, and want others to see that importance too, yet they aren't completely sure of how to create the one they envision.

In Chapter 2 we defined culture as "the way we do things around here," and in Chapter 3 we talked about the fact that everyone owns the culture. Given all of that, you might wonder why we are playing the

C-suite card here. If we all own the culture, why is the opening story about a CEO?

Although we totally agree that culture is co-owned by everyone (and as you will see, we also believe it should be consciously co-created), we have to start somewhere. If you are in senior leadership, this chapter is for you—we are talking about an overall process for defining an aspirational macroculture. The next chapter helps you apply this same process to defining the microculture of any team. If your organization is ten to fifteen people, these two cultures might be one and the same. The bigger your organization, the more complex this becomes, but the thinking behind the process won't change.

The Underlying Truths

Two important truths are hiding in plain sight in the title of this chapter. Getting your team on board with these truths is as buying in yourself. Until everyone sees and understands these things, you will have understandable, but unnecessary, resistance.

- *Truth 1:* We can define and design a culture. Yes, culture exists naturally, but a group/team can consciously shift and change that culture. It won't change instantly or by magic, but it can be intentionally altered.

- *Truth 2:* If we are going to change it, why not go big? Don't put a limit on your aspirations. Once you realize you can define (and change) your culture, you can define what you want. There's no need to settle for incremental improvement.

In a world of distance work in which so many feel culture is less clear or unstable, and less able to be controlled/influenced, these are increasingly important truths.

The Culture Definition Process

In this chapter we outline a process for defining and creating the culture you desire. Before we share detailed information, here is a high-level view of the steps.

1. *Determine your moment.* You can define an aspirational culture at any time, but determining the right moment to create an inflection point is important. If you know a re-organization is pending, if you have had a lot of turnover on the team, or if new leadership is taking over, you may already have your inflection point. These may be the moments you are looking for—or they will help you determine when the best time might be.

2. *Communicate the reasons/start the process.* Everyone needs to understand why you are changing and why it matters. Moving toward an aspirational vision should be seen as change—because it is one. And this is how you begin.

3. *Create a team.* Determine who you will bring together to do the initial work and define your expectations of that group.

4. *Paint the picture.* Determine the team's picture of a perfect working culture and begin to see it.

5. *Draft the cultural vision.* Once you have the picture, the team must put it into words so others see it in the same way.

6. *Socialize and revise.* Since not everyone was involved in creating the vision and statement, you must gain feedback to improve the vision and engage the team in discussion.

7. *Finalize and formally communicate the vision.* An aspirational culture needs words associated with it. This is where you finalize the draft. Once it is finalized, share it widely.

8. *Refine microcultures.* Once the organization defines the future of the culture, teams can continue the conversations themselves (more in Chapter 9).

9. *Operationalize it.* It is one thing to determine what the desired culture is; it is something else to make it happen. This is the focus of Chapter 10.

Let's dive in . . .

1. Determine Your Moment

Stephano feels the need for a shift. If you are feeling that intuition too, listen to it, but that doesn't necessarily mean you should start this process tomorrow. As is true for the introduction of any major initiative and change (and this is both), timing matters. Think about the seasonality of your business; for example, if you are retail or a public accounting firm, you certainly wouldn't want to be distracted from the natural peaks in the business some times of the year. Or if you and the organization are weary from significant change, you might want to wait. If the merger was announced last week, for instance, it is too soon. But if the pain of culture has been around for a while, search for the right time rather than just saying "we can't do it now."

If you are a senior leader, start talking about what you are seeing and feeling and how you need to adjust the culture to understand your team members' acceptance and commitment level, as well as gain a collective sense of when to initiate this effort.

2. Communicate the Reasons/Start the Process

Some of these reasons might be behind your desire to redefine culture in the first place:

- A merger or acquisition

- A major change in the marketplace
- Major changes in leadership (especially if there are style differences)
- Talent retention problems
- Morale or engagement issues

While these or other reasons might be clear to you and are what point you toward wanting to redefine/reimagine your culture, it is critical that you communicate this initiative to the organization. As a leader, you have a different perspective—others don't necessarily see or value things that you see in the same way.

Consider this step as a way to provide the context for others to understand why, and why now, you need to change the culture of this work.

It is important to note that some may see this change as welcome ("It is about time we worked on culture!"), others may see it as unnecessary ("Our culture is fine—it's not any worse than anyplace else I've worked."), and still others may see it as ridiculous ("You aren't really going to change that stuff around here!"). Chances are you will have all three views represented in the organization. You may even have people who truly don't care about culture—they are simply working a job and don't feel any desire to change things. For example, contractors often feel they aren't "really" part of the team and work as if they are completely detached. That is why, as in any change effort, clearly defining the current situation and the reasons for looking at the culture are so important. People who have felt uninspired or disengaged before may change the way they look at their teammates and their connection to the organization.

3. Create a Team

If your organization is of any size, you will need a representative team to start this work. Your role is to raise the issue at the right time, announce the need to redefine culture (and explain why), then provide resources and participate, but not dominate or lead the effort. This can't be Stephano's (or your) culture; it must belong to the team. Creating a team for this effort involves identifying who is on the team, setting clear expectations of that team, and providing a process through which they can provide their input.

In our experience the team should consist of

- *People who want to be involved.* You want to recruit initial champions of change and those who are passionate about this work. Start with volunteers.

- *People who represent the whole organization.* Work from the list of volunteers to create a cross section of demographics, parts of the organization, and organizational level.

- *People who represent the group.* This team can bring their opinions, but they must think like representatives, not individuals. Ultimately the vision will go back to the larger organization and this team will play a big role in communicating the first draft and getting feedback.

- *The senior leader/sponsor.* That person, perhaps it is you, should participate in the conversations as a member, not as the leader.

- *Not more than twenty-ish people.* If the group gets too big, the process will become unwieldly. While fewer than this is great for many group-dynamics reasons, for work of this type, scope, and importance, you will likely want a few more.

- *A facilitator.* This will likely be someone from outside of the team or organization who can remain neutral and focus on the process. They should bring good facilitation skills and hopefully a good understanding of the goals and process we are outlining here.

Chances are, you will have more volunteers than spots on the team (if not, your culture may have bigger issues than you realize). You will want to thank them, perhaps collect some ideas from them before the team meets, and use them in Step 6 of this process.

4. Paint the Picture

Next, bring this highly motivated group together to begin creating an aspirational culture for your organization/team. Your goal is to create a draft vision of the collective aspirational culture. It will necessarily need to be in words, but much symbolism and depth will be behind those words. This means you don't start by only drafting some bullet points, but by seeing a three-dimensional picture of a future state. Too often people try to use only words. The more you can include images, pictures, stories, models, and metaphors, the more real and powerful the words will become. You will want to lean on your consultant and/or facilitator to develop the details, but here are some of the components of this event and the tools you will use:

- Review the context and reasons for doing this (restate Step 2), and clarify the goals for this interactive and open session.

- Create a chance for participants to share ideas openly and encourage open minds. In order to get a good start, it will be important for people to feel safe to stretch their minds and withhold judgment.

- Include exercises and *multisensory approaches* to paint a picture of the perfect culture for your organization. Spend time seeing and talking about that picture before moving to words too quickly.

5. Draft the Cultural Vision

After the dream and visioning phase, you must work to capture the vision and turn those ideas into meaningful words. Although your specific words will come from the team's work, use the 3C Model to help make sure you are creating a full and complete picture of the culture you aspire to.

Wordsmithing can be tedious, but much of this work is important. (This is another reason why you need a skilled facilitator). Remember what Socrates said: *The beginning of wisdom is the definition of terms.* What the terms are matter far less than how clearly they are understood by this group and can be shared with the broader organization.

Moreover, the final document will reflect the feeling of those involved in crafting it, but what about those who come in after the initial work is done? Will they understand and be able to appreciate what kind of team they've joined and how to succeed in it? Make sure you have a way to transfer the feeling behind the words to those who weren't directly involved in the process.

Remember that the goal is to create an exciting, clear picture of an aspirational culture in words. The statement should be clear, real, and succinct. The more real the language (and less it feels like corporate speak) the more powerful, effective, and understood it will be. If it is longer than a page, it is too long.

One more thing about the session(s) that create Steps 4 and 5—done well, this process will create energy and anticipation, and likely it will be a manifestation of many of the features of the culture you are trying to describe. Kevin has talked to people several years after these meetings who still speak fondly and passionately about these meetings. When the team leaves feeling a palpable energy about their work product, the next steps will go far more smoothly.

Most likely the goal isn't to throw everything about the current culture out of the window. Although you want a picture of a desired future, you likely want to maintain some things about your culture (maybe a lot). Make sure this group—and the rest of the organization—sees what is great and will continue, as well as what they should aspire to. Stated another way—when you examine the draft statement, you will be closer to your goal on some parts than others.

6. Socialize and Revise

Once the draft is created, it needs to be widely shared and socialized. How you accomplish this will vary widely based on the size and complexity of your organization. Use any past examples of success in communicating change as your guide. Think of ways you can involve both the core team and those who volunteered to help create the vision but who weren't selected as core team members in this process. Include them in this next step in meaningful ways and consider them as change agents throughout the rest of this process. Reward and use their energy and interest.

The goal isn't for the team to present the draft aspiration culture as completed work, because it isn't. Rather, the goal is to share it and the meaning behind it. After this is done, those sharing (presumably the core team) should ask for questions and feedback on both the vision itself and the words used to describe it.

Getting this feedback is important for these reasons:

- *The final vision will get better.* As you get feedback the language will become clearer and more inclusive.

- *Interest and energy will grow.* Asking for feedback will raise energy and interest in the process and show people that the organization is serious about this effort.

- *Ownership will grow.* Giving people input helps to raise their feelings of ownership. After all, you are trying to create a collective vision, not one that came from a small group in a conference room.

- *Anticipation will grow.* People will begin to get excited about this future state! Even the most cynical will see value in moving toward the vision being presented.

- *Change will start.* You begin to move hearts and minds. Remember that you and the core team have greater understanding and acceptance then everyone else. It is easy to falsely assume that other people see what you see. Taking this widespread socialization step will help overcome this.

Consider both synchronous and asynchronous ways to socialize the idea. Certainly, live descriptions and discussions of the vision are helpful, but make sure you are recording these and giving everyone in the organization, even those working remotely, the chance to share their ideas, input, and questions. Use your technology tools like channels and forums to assist. Remember, though, that the richer the discussion and the more people who feel they have a chance to provide input, the quicker you will gain stronger commitment to the vision.

7. Finalize and Formally Communicate the Vision

Now that you've gathered the organizational feedback, you can update the initial draft. Although you could bring the entire group back to do this, you might want to use a subset of the original team or have the entire team meet in an asynchronous or virtual way. Use your past organizational experience to create a process that works here.

Once you have your final product, communicate it widely. Chances are you have experienced something being communicated from above in an organization. Whether you loved the idea or not, it probably felt very hollow if an implementation plan wasn't associated with it. Don't leave people excited about a vision but confused about what's happening next.

Final Thoughts

Creating an aspirational culture for your team or organization can be exciting, but make sure to treat it as the organizational change effort that it is. It isn't a new software system or a process change; it is actually bigger! It is the start of a reworking and rewiring of the organization—literally, how we do things—that can create greater organizational success far into the future.

Chapter 9

Building the Micro Inside the Macro

Luisa wants to make a difference. She has always been proactive in trying to make things better. That proactivity played a big role in her promotion into her first leadership role. Now she wants to take aim at improving the culture of her team. She realizes that not everyone thinks they can change it and so they feel it is a waste of time to even talk about it. Because it is a hybrid team, many of the folks who don't go into the office don't think it's as important as those who go in every day feel it is. In fact, they almost act as if they are a separate team entirely. Yet Luisa sees that a stronger microculture can become a significant advantage for the team, and for her career too. Due to both her nature and her experience, she doesn't want to wait. It's time to reform the team's culture.

Maybe you can relate to Luisa. If so, this chapter is for you. Or maybe you are a bit more reticent than she is—you know that changing your team's culture could be helpful, but you aren't as eager or confident. This chapter is for you too because once you are equipped with a plan and know you don't have to do it alone, you will be ready to move forward.

Where We Are Headed

You know culture is important, and you probably realize that cultures aren't all the same from location to location, team to team and region to region. All of that can be okay—there is room for differences. We can be as intentional about creating a microculture as we are about the organization's culture as a whole. The goal, then, is to intentionally create a valuable microculture that is connected and aligned with the macroculture.

What if you are Luisa and the organization isn't approaching this issue in the same way? Say your team has a reputation for being slow to respond to requests because they are concerned about making sure everything is properly documented. In this instance, you have a conflict between the macroculture and your team's microculture. When you are aware of disconnects like these, you are better able to determine if you should wait or be proactive in addressing your microculture.

We suggest you move forward, knowing that what you create might become a positive force for change in the larger organization. Most likely you have room to define your microculture even if the macroculture isn't completely defined. Even without a clear definition or an aspirational vision, the macroculture exists. And when what you create gets great results, people in the rest of the organization will notice.

In Chapter 3, we thoroughly discussed (and hopefully persuaded you to realize) how if you are the team leader, you have tremendous influence on your team's microculture. Even if you're reading this as a teammate with no positional power, know that you are a part of the culture and can influence it. Keep that in mind as you read on.

Conceptually we are going to apply the same culture definition process we introduced in the last chapter here, but you will need to address some important differences in context. If you need to review the steps, refer back to Chapter 8.

Determine Your Moment

If you are Luisa, the time to start is now regardless of what is going on in the larger organization. The sooner you and your team can coalesce around a shared aspirational culture, the sooner the team can begin moving toward it. You might want to pump the brakes rather than mash down the accelerator in some situations though. Consider these questions:

- *Are other major changes going on in the organization now (or are any forthcoming)?* If so, waiting for those to be implemented or at least understood is likely the right choice.

- *Is the larger organization undertaking conversations about culture?* If so, wait for those to settle out first (more on this in a bit).

- *How strong is your team's microculture already?* Yes, it can likely be improved, but is this effort the best (highest leveraged) use of your time, effort, and focus now?

Assuming none of these red flags exist, now might be/probably is a great time to work on defining your team's microculture.

Communicate the Reasons/Start the Process

To gain the impact and commitment you need from everyone (and the resulting cultural vision), you must communicate the purpose, and understand and address your team's questions and concerns. Be ready to answer questions like these:

- Why do you feel that now is the time to work on culture?

- What factors lead you to this conclusion?

- Why is this worth the effort?

- Will the larger organization support our efforts?

How you start this process is important to your success. Although you aren't defining the culture for the team (and we won't presume we know where you are headed), we are confident that you want more commitment, more collaboration, and high trust in your microculture. Communicating and getting people on board with this work is a way to model the types of things you want to see in your future culture.

Create a Team

In the process we outlined in the previous chapter this step was important—to find and build a team from the larger organization. In defining a microculture, depending on the size of your team, this might mean that everyone will be involved directly. If your group is larger, you might be thinking about this work for a region, division, large facility, or other large group. If so, that is great. Look back to the previous chapter, as the advice around larger groups there will apply to you here. (And know that you might have smaller working teams do further microculture work later). But if your team is fewer than fifteen to twenty people, we encourage you to enlist and welcome the help of everyone in this process.

Paint the Picture

The goal is to create a three-dimensional picture of the desired microculture. This visual should get the team excited, both for the way people will feel and for how productive and successful the team will be. The steps outlined in the last chapter apply here too.

Where should you start? Do you start with your microculture vision, or do you start with the organizational picture? Because you know that alignment is important in the end, it might seem convenient and efficient to start with the macroculture. But before we jump to that assumption, let's look at several questions.

- *Does a macroculture vision exist?* If not, it is pretty hard to start there.

- *Will the macroculture vision stunt us?* Yes, you ultimately need alignment, but if you start by looking too closely at the macroculture vision, will you simply agree and approve it? If so, you won't likely have had the conversation that will make your microculture your own, and ultimately, as powerful as it could be.

- *Can we use the macroculture statement as a guide?* We suggest you quickly review the statement for style and approach, then put it aside and focus on what you need on your team.

Once you have decided the role of a macroculture vision, you can begin to personalize the picture for your team. Ask questions like these:

- What do we want work to look and feel like?

- How do we want to interact?

- What attributes and characteristics of the team and our work will lead to great results?

- How would we describe the place we would most like to work?

- What would the perfect working environment and culture look like?

Asking yourself, and your teammates, these types of questions will allow you to have the deep and exciting conversations that will help you create a compelling and exciting picture of your future culture.

After your discussions and conversations, it is time to draft some words to describe that vision. Use words that are clear, simple, and don't sound like corporate-ese.

If you are looking for specific examples here, you may be a little disappointed. We are typically cautious about showing a sample statement too early because people tend to get enamored with the words and statements of others and don't do the work to create meaningful statements for themselves.

Socialize and Revise

If you did the previous step with the entire team, you have no one to socialize this vision with, but the adage of sleeping on a decision applies here. It is very possible that the team will be very excited when they leave the session where words have been selected to document the aspirational cultural vision. Although you want all that energy and engagement—especially in something like this—take a little time to let it settle and to reflect on its value.

Provide multiple ways—on and offline, synchronously, and asynchronously—for people to provide input and ask questions. This gives everyone ample opportunity to contribute and avoids groupthink or getting caught up in the energy of the moment. Remember that it might be important to provide an anonymous way to share ideas in order to avoid peer pressure or groupthink. Schedule another session in which you look at the vision again to make sure everyone still feels great about it and no new questions have emerged.

Align and Confirm

If you do have a macroculture statement, now is the time to carefully align your words with that vision. The primary question here is this: Does our microculture statement align with that larger statement?

The fact that you have created your own statement is important, but it cannot be at cross purposes with the larger organizational vision. Here is a simple and obvious example. If it is clear from the macro vision that the culture will be focused on teamwork and collaboration, but your microcultural vision is focused on independence and individual contribution, you have a problem.

Your words and the meanings behind them matter. We do not believe your words need to match or copy the macroculture vision; if we did, we wouldn't suggest building your own. But the statements/visions must clearly align.

Spend the time necessary to find the alignment and make any changes to the language of your vision to make sure that alignment exists.

Finalize and Formally Communicate

Once you have agreement and alignment, it's time to finalize your vision. Again, if your team is small, and all have been involved in the creation process, there isn't much to this step. But if you are doing this on a larger department or regional scale, the advice in the previous chapter on this step applies to you.

Operationalize It

The next chapter will help you with some detailed suggestions about how to make your vision your reality, and it is important that you follow those steps and ideas. There is tremendous power in the work you have done up to this point. In our experience, if you have followed the steps until now in an open and inclusive way, the process itself has likely moved you in the direction of your cultural vision—regardless of how you have defined it.

However, if people see this work as a gesture, or hollow work that isn't followed up, the trust and engagement levels you are likely hoping to promote may crash to lower levels than you experienced before you began. And the more of the time your team works remotely, the bigger the risk.

As you worked on creating this cultural vision together, whether you were physically together or not, you created positive energy and momentum. The team became more aligned than perhaps the team was previously.

Just as in our personal lives, promises repeatedly made and broken will eventually erode trust. Your team likely won't give you many chances, so you need to get this right.

Final Thoughts

We want you to think about what will work for you and your team. And we can say with assurance that if you do this work and apply the ideas in the two chapters that follow, your culture will shift and improve and many good things will come from those efforts.

And...

You must remember that you are doing this work in the context of a larger organization. Share your successes across the organization and, trust us, they will be positively noticed. But don't get smug or self-aggrandizing. Use your successes to spread the word and the practices that have worked for you to create greater good in the organization.

Remote and hybrid work often create an insular situation where the "nuclear" team (your immediate colleagues) is very connected and knows what's happening, but those on other teams or those in other locations aren't aware of what's going on in your team's world.

You can be the proof of concept others need to make changes of their own. Sharing your success can give you and your team's efforts real visibility and inspire others, no matter where they are located. When you share, you will be leading the way to a brighter future—regardless of what your job title says today.

Chapter 10

Making the Culture Come to Life

Carey and her team have created a cultural vision for their team and they're excited that it aligns with the vision created by the larger organization. It is motivating and exhilarating, but they don't really know how to move from where they are now to their desired future. It was easy to create the vision, but now that it is time to do the work, they are motivated but aren't sure how to start.

Although working through the process of creating a vision may not be easy (especially getting agreement on the words), it is, likely, pretty exciting. In fact, if you've been following along and now have a cultural vision, and you and the team aren't excited about it, something is probably wrong with the statement. If you haven't generated energy and excitement about the future you've created together, your chances of getting there are slim.

Everything that follows in this chapter assumes you have a culture statement that people see as aspirational—a description of a working situation they want to be in and would thrive in. Once you have such a vision and statement, the real work begins.

Translating Vision into Reality

Remember that a culture doesn't belong to the organization or the manager, but to everyone, and therefore everyone has a role to play in bringing it to life. After all, since culture is "how we do things here," everyone is doing things now, some of which will need to change to reach your cultural vision. Fundamentally, we are talking about a change effort here, but don't worry, we won't get into change models or esoteric thinking; we'll be practical about what needs to happen and how everyone plays a role.

Everything we discuss in this chapter applies to both macroculture and microculture, because it is all culture—it is all about "how we do things." Apply these ideas in a way that makes sense in your situation.

The Components of Nurturing Your Culture

These components will help you move from a wonderful statement to daily activities:

- *Behaviors.* What everyone is truly doing regularly defines and describes the culture, but what are the behaviors we need to reach our lofty goals?

- *Expectations.* What we expect of each other defines and reinforces the culture too. Ask yourself: What does our desired culture imply about what we should expect from each other? Is it different when we are working together or separately?

- *Skills*. If your desired culture is a stretch from where you are now, what skills will people need to achieve that future? How can we help each other build those skills?

- *Agreements*. Agreements close the loop on the day-to-day activities. These agreements can create and solidify accountability to answer important questions: How will you treat and interact with each other? When and how do we communicate on a Long-Distance Team? How do we deal with synchronous and asynchronous communication across multiple time zones? Carey and her people might agree to provide regular asynchronous updates to reduce the number of meetings. Teams that use chat groups as an electronic logbook can keep everyone informed regardless of their time zone or when flexibility takes them outside "normal" work hours.

- *Decisions*. Decisions, big and small, made by everyone, but especially by leaders, are the backbone of a culture. How do we use our aspirational culture as a lens for making good decisions?

- *Measures*. Measuring progress and success of important initiatives is critical. How will we know where we are and when we have arrived?

These are interconnected and self-reinforcing steps, but we will look at each separately to move tangibly from the culture you have to the culture you want. Although these steps would be the same for any cultural transformation, each has unique challenges and specific nuances we must consider in a long-distance working situation.

Although we don't know what your aspirational culture statement is, we will try to give examples in each step that you will recognize and that might even align with the culture you are trying to create.

Behaviors That Define the New Culture

If our aspirational culture is where we want to go, it is behaviors that will let us know that we arrived. We must translate the shiny statement into actions. Start with questions like these:

- What will this culture look like in real time?

- How will this culture play out when we aren't physically together?

- What do we all need to do to make this culture our reality?

- What do I personally need to do?

Brainstorm these questions and capture specific ideas. This is how you begin the process of translating a great idea into action. You can achieve this in a traditional brainstorming session—either in person or via a meeting platform—but we suggest you do it in a blended way. Pose the questions to individuals and have them think about their answers, being as specific as possible before having a synchronous conversation. Specificity and clarity are too important to leave to the popcorn-popping nature of a brainstorming session that people either aren't prepared for or don't have a chance to think about in a calm manner.

Although you want people to think about the more personal question ("What do I personally need to do?"), let them know they don't have to share all their answers to this question with the group if they don't want to. Questions like this might lead people to feel defensive and that won't help the process.

Let's say your aspirational culture desires/requires high levels of trust across the team. If you start talking about the trust behaviors you will need to exhibit, many people will feel like they are exhibiting them, and they may be—part of the time! Culture isn't what happens when we are all our best selves, but what our everyday selves do. To overcome any possible defensiveness, talk about it upfront. The truth is, if we model the behaviors we want, even some of the time, it gives us hope we can achieve the culture we want.

The goal is to create a complete list of desired behaviors without considering positions or rank. The list may include things like proactivity, transparency, and respectfully challenging ideas. Everyone is a creator of the culture, and although leaders or senior leaders will have opinions too, they shouldn't go first or carry extra weight. Once you have this list, even in draft form, you can begin working on the other components.

Expectations That Reinforce the New Culture

It's hard to overstate the connection between clear expectations and success at work. In a long-distance–work world, the need for expectations grows even more important. That is why we are devoting Chapter 11 to this activity. Although we will leave the details of expectation setting to that chapter, there are some specifics here we need to clarify.

Usually expectations focus on

- What the leader expects from team members
- What defines successful delivery of the work

Although both are important, they are far from a full understanding or description of what expectations at work can be or need to be. While expectations define success in the core work, to support and create the culture we want, we must include "How will we live the culture?" as a part of that success.

For example, if your new culture points to strong relationships, what does that mean to individuals? You will need to have a conversation about that point and then set expectations about how to build and maintain those relationships within your team. Much of that will fall into the realm of clear expectations. Is it okay to stop by a desk for a coffee break? Or have a virtual coffee? Are you expected to build relationships with everyone, not just those you work most closely with or those who are in the office on the same days as you? And how far out do you need to extend these great relationships? Should they include our internal customers and suppliers or just our nuclear team?

Everyone has a role—not just leaders—in defining and understanding expectations. Doing this well creates many positive outcomes, including helping the team move more quickly toward the desired culture.

Skills Required to Live the New Culture

Since culture is ultimately about what we do, a natural question is this: Are we able to do all those things? Perhaps the most undervalued component in creating your aspirational culture is understanding the skills that will be needed, and then making sure everyone has them. If your culture requires people to be flexible and agile, people must know what that entails (behavior) and how to achieve it as well. Depending on their experience, they may not be used to acting without explicit signoff. There is a difference between knowing something and being able to apply that knowledge, and that is where skills come in.

In our experience with clients, once the culture is defined, one of the most powerful things you can do is determine what skills people need to achieve the desired culture. Chances are this will reveal some skill gaps. Perhaps the gaps are technical in nature—like how to use some of the more undervalued features on your meeting platform to get better engagement, or how to use interpersonal skills like listening and communicating whether in-person or via webcams.

Say your culture values open communication. We've all built relationships before, and we know they require trust and transparency. Some of the skills that demonstrate those values in a distributed team might be using webcams for one-on-one conversations or using your collaboration tool to contribute to high-value discussions. (You know your team better than we do. These are examples.) What common skills sets will help you reach your desired culture more quickly and more sustainably?

The skill development might be intense and take some time. More likely, it will simply involve helping people use the "blur background" button or background visuals so their home clutter isn't apparent to their teammates.

Not everyone is comfortable documenting their thoughts this way. Although tools like Microsoft Teams may be intuitive to some, they are intimidating or awkward for others. Many people will need training in their effective use, which may range from job aids and reminders, to peer coaching, to actual training on the software.

You can translate your cultural statement into a list of skills for both macro- and microcultures. On the macroculture level, we recommend getting your Training or Learning and Development (L&D) professionals involved; they can help you ask the right questions and build a skill list. On the microculture level, the team can create this list, or they can be assisted by someone in Training, Learning, or HR. Getting such help may save you time and will likely give you more confidence in the result, but there is another important reason for getting this outside perspective.

Having a list of required skills is fine, but how will you build them? Having your learning professionals on your side in this effort allows them to bring more of their expertise to the table. They can help you determine how you will build these skills across the team or organization.

As a leadership and learning organization, The Kevin Eikenberry Group has long been in the business of designing and creating learning tools and experiences for individual and organizations. A quick look on our website will show you that we provide both synchronous and asynchronous learning options, as well as everything from eLearning to a wide variety of virtual and in-person learning approaches. Although all of these may have a place in building the skills needed to support your culture, we believe multiple benefits come from synchronous learning experiences, and if possible, face-to-face learning. The right answer for every team is a blend that addresses their specific needs. Choose what works best for you.

In any skill-building situation with a group of people, not everyone will have the same needs. The skill gap will be larger for some than it is for others based on experience, opportunities, and knowledge. When the skills gaps vary, it makes sense to offer more tailored skill building for certain individuals. When building skills(s) across a team, regardless of job role or experience, to support culture, there is another important factor to consider.

When you bring people together to collectively learn a skill or skills as a team, and when you do this in the context of supporting the culture, magic can happen. Remember, *together* doesn't necessarily mean in the same room at the same time (although don't discount the power of that). Virtual Instructor Led Trainings (VILTs) create similar social learning opportunities as traditional classroom instruction, even if the catering isn't as good.

Yes, you have the chance to improve your work, but you also have the chance to build the camaraderie, trust, and relationships that will more broadly strengthen the team and the culture at the same time. Having people together (and yes, if possible, we mean in-person) to build skills and collectively work on those skills in service of improving culture can bring the group together.

You will likely use a mixture of approaches to build the skills of the group—both collectively and individually—and that is wise. Role plays can be done through webcam and breakout rooms in Zoom or Microsoft Teams. Prework and "think time" can happen where people are at any time so that when they assemble at the same time, they're ready to get to work. Don't discount the power and energy that can come from having a group work together on those needed skills and to build the culture at the same time.

Agreements to Create Accountability for the New Culture

If John is saying (or even just thinking), "Look at what Sandy is doing. That isn't the culture we talked about," several things may be going on:

- John may be right, but even if he is wrong, he is clearly questioning Sandy's intentions.

- Trust is reduced.

- The chances for conflict—and a cultural reversal—are increased.

And those aren't the only things people will be thinking, questioning, or making assumptions about. If you have a hybrid team, cliques of people might form among those in the office or in the office on the same days. These people may have no ill intent, and in fact, they may be more engaged because of those relationships, but how do those not included feel? If you were ever "outside" of a clique or group in school, you know the answer.

We think of agreements as shared group expectations. They can help you reduce misunderstandings, clear up intent, and most importantly, create mutual accountability for and positive peer pressure in everyone living the culture you want.

In Chapter 12 we will describe how to create these agreements in detail and how to have them accelerate progress toward the culture you desire.

Decisions That Refine the New Culture

While everyone on the team makes decisions, this component is mostly focused on leaders because they are often making the larger, more momentous decisions that impact the entire team. When the team looks at a decision (and its implications) and sees it conflicting with the desired culture, it can be a huge blow to cultural progress. Whether the decisions are strategic or tactical, the team will scrutinize each one, considering the cultural implications.

And it isn't just the decisions themselves but how you reach them that will matter. People are looking at the decision and the decision-making process and assuming (rightly or not) the leader's intent. This has always been true, but once you all agree on the way to work together, the pressure is on leaders at all levels to make sure everyone acts in alignment with the new culture.

In a long-distance working situation, this can be even more evident, and more disastrous if you do it wrong. Even in the "old days" when "corporate" made a decision, it was often better received by those in that building with access to and greater trust in the leaders than it was out in the rest of the organization. That will still be true for the macroculture (though it might be even more complex now), but for the microculture of a hybrid team, that same scenario can occur between those in the office (or in the office regularly) and those who aren't.

We aren't talking about spinning communication or simply looking at the optics of the decision either. We are suggesting that decisions get made through the lens of the culture. The basic question to ask is this:

What is the right decision when looking through the lens of the culture we want?

This sounds great and like a tidy solution, but in that real world, decisions are often complex. Sometimes a single decision will have multiple implications. In our experience, looking at the decisions through the lens of the culture first creates better long-term decisions and creates a way to communicate the decisions in a way that is consistent with, and allows for conversation about, the cultural implications. Being open about decision making maintains and raises trust.

Although we started by saying this component is more about leaders, everyone else isn't exempt. When all of us make decisions about what to do, how to treat others, and more, thinking about that same question, *What is the right decision to make when we specifically think of the culture we want?* we will be moving in the right direction.

Measures to Track Progress and Success

The old line of what gets measured gets done, while simplistic, is accurate. Here is where you are: you have a culture, and you have one you want. How will you measure where you are, and how will you know when you have achieved your objective?

The most common answer to this question is the employee engagement survey. And without question, it can be a part of this process. If you have one that you use organizationally, great. Even better if you can tweak or modify it to ask questions that gauge progress toward this new cultural vision. If you are using an "out of the box" tool, make sure it allows you to clearly assess progress toward your cultural vision. If it does not, it is time to talk to your assessment vendor or provider to make the needed adjustments or add the needed questions. If they aren't willing to help, create an addendum, or find a new partner.

Most of these tools allow you to slice and dice the data to see how individual teams (and leaders) are doing on these dimensions. Assuming the assessment is aligned with your goals, this allows you to measure snapshots of both macro- and microculture. Since each assessment is just a snapshot, you will want to implement an ongoing process of measurement to help you look at progress.

What if you are looking at your microculture and either there isn't an organizational assessment, or it isn't hitting the mark? Then you can look for other ways to measure progress. Here are some ideas to consider:

- Have the team do an assessment in open conversation.

- Have an internal (Human Resources/Organizational Development/Learning and Development) resource or an external consultant/partner do focus groups or a tailored anonymous survey.

- Include questions about cultural progress in exit and stay interviews.

- Ask questions about cultural progress in team meetings, one-on-ones, or formal performance management conversations.

Chances are you will want to use more than one of these ways (or others you identify) to continually assess your progress. Not everyone will feel the same way, and sentiment and experience will change over time (particular successes or failures might sway thoughts at a given time), which is why we need to keep asking.

Culture is ever evolving, and we must continue to assess progress in both formal and informal ways.

Final Thoughts

How will you know you have reached your aspirational culture? Certainly, the measures will help. And when you develop a truly aspirational culture, you may never fully arrive (and that is okay). But when people start questioning why you are calling it the "new culture," and suggest you simply call it our culture, you know you are getting close. Although it will always be a journey, when people achieve the new as the norm, are clear on what that means, and expect it from each other, you should celebrate your progress. Using the components outlined in this chapter will help you get there sooner.

Part V

Applying Core Principles

You will want more tools in your toolkit to help you support, maintain, and nurture the teams and culture you have created. They aren't new, but we consistently see them underutilized and even misapplied. When you and your team learn how to apply these tools, you will be able to maintain what you have designed but also adapt and adjust to changing conditions around you.

Chapter 11

Applying the Power of Expectations

Sara is a mid-level leader who is excited about reinforcing and making the microculture her team has envisioned come to life. She knows everyone wants to make the adjustments but also knows it requires everyone to change their behavior. She wonders how she and the whole team can find ways to remind each other to do what they profess to want. She asks, Is there a way to use a tool that already exists, and that people are familiar with, to do this?

Yes, Sara, there is.

The simple answer is that well-selected and set expectations are a major tool for reinforcing the behaviors that constitute the culture you want. Although all of us are familiar with the term *expectations* and have some experience in setting and using them, we have some work to do to unleash the full power of their value for leaders like Sara and everyone on their teams.

Traditionally, when people think about expectations at work, they think about the expectations that the boss (like Sara) has of her direct reports. These expectations are critically important, but they are not the only expectations that matter. First off, expectations run both ways, so although Sara rightly needs expectations of her team members, the team members have expectations of her as well. Expectations should be considered between team members both in general and on specific projects or situations.

Why Expectations Matter

Expectations define success in any situation. Once we know what is expected of us, we know where the bar or standard of excellence is, but that isn't enough. Expectations must be mutually clear for both parties. It is one thing for you as a leader to know what you expect, but if the team member doesn't understand or has a different understanding, the power of the expectation is lost. And lastly, once the expectations are set and mutually clear, there is the matter of belief. Do people believe they can achieve that expectation?

Think of a time when you had a role or job and were confident you understood and agreed with what your boss expected of you. When you envision that situation (maybe it is right now—and if so, congratulations), you will notice that . . .

- *You have greater confidence.* Even if you don't yet believe you can achieve the expectation, when you are clear and can focus on achieving it, your confidence grows (and with increased confidence, you are more likely to meet the expectation).

- *You experience greater trust.* The process of creating clear expectations with someone requires and creates more trust. When we experience that with our boss, it is doubly valuable.

- *There is less workplace conflict and frustration.* Our review of the literature shows that unclear roles and expectations are always cited as causes of workplace conflict. In our personal work, we see these as the most prevalent. And even if a mismatch between you and your boss doesn't become conflict, both of you can experience general frustration.

- *There is less rework.* Perhaps this is the most obvious. Have you ever delivered something to someone thinking it was exactly what they needed, only to be told you needed to adjust/rework/redo it? If so, you know that if the expectation had been mutually clear to start with, you wouldn't have needed to rework anything.

- *There is less micromanagement.* There's no doubt that many leaders micromanage. When they trust that people know what they want, they will be less likely to need to constantly check-in, and when employees trust their manager, their interactions feels less like micromanagement.

Add to this impressive list that when expectations are clear, you get better results.

How Expectations Drive Culture

You can look to the preceding list as proof that setting clear expectations is good management/leadership practice (and it is). But look at it again through the lens of culture. Whatever your vision is of your future culture, we are confident it doesn't include more conflict, more rework, more frustration, and more micromanagement. None of those things support a working environment people want.

But there is more to the expectations/culture connection. Whatever the expectations of the work, regardless of how clear they are, they send a message to everyone about what is expected around here. That means they're a mirror image of the current culture. When we create new expectations that coincide with the new culture, we are reinforcing and intentionally thinking about the daily activities and approaches that will create it.

Areas of Expectations

As you have been reading, we're confident you have been thinking about at least one part of the expectation mosaic. Actually, we need to consider three types of expectations, both to create desired culture and to reflect the more complex nature of a long-distance–work situation. They are the "what, why, and how," of the work.

The "What" of the Work

When we think of expectations, we usually think about the quality of the work product and the timing and delivery of that work—in other words, the specifics of the work and the details of the job description. These expectations are the foundation of work success and what leaders must be able to do. We have plenty of stories that support the notion that although this is a foundational skill, many leaders aren't doing it well at all. Ironically, even though this is what many of us think of when we talk about expectations, the task descriptions are ultimately least important to our culture conversation.

The "Why" of the Work

Why is this work being done? Who uses the output and for what purpose? The "why" expectations provide the context and meaning for the work and help people use their judgement and experience to deliver better results. Have you ever been asked to do a task without this context? You might deliver it, but you likely have little commitment to it beyond personal pride. But if you know how Josephine uses what you do, and you know and care about Josephine, everything changes. The why expectations are critical to your desired culture because we can assume that culture cares about relationships. Further, if you work at a distance and don't know the whys, or you don't know Josephine very well, you will likely view your work as your work and not think about yourself as a part of the larger team.

The "How" of the Work

The "how" expectations are a direct shot at culture. Do people know the expectations around communication, collaboration, and cohesion (the 3Cs)? Are the work processes and flows clearly understood and discussed? Do these expectations match up with the culture? If not, it is time to reassess and reset them. In a long-distance work situation, these considerations are more important than ever because people have fewer clues to figure it out through observation.

As a leader it is important for you to be great at setting and managing expectations in all three of these areas. Even if you have done this well in the past, things change. Let's say you get a new system that eliminates steps in your carefully laid-out workflow. Or a new regulation adds a step and slows the work a bit. As your working situation, team design, and aspirational cultural change, you need to reexamine and reconfirm expectations.

How to Set Them

Setting clear expectations follows a pretty easy process, though there are perils in each of the steps.

1. *Make them clear yourself.* Before you can set expectations with someone, you must be clear on them yourself. This sounds obvious, but what is floating around in your head is seldom clear enough yet. Think about each type of expectation and write down what you really want to see on the job. Writing it down will create your initial clarity.

2. *Talk it out.* Thoughts are fuzzy and words bring clarity. Take your written thoughts and talk them out. Don't simply read them, but explain them to a friend, your spouse, or your pet. Notice how you further clarify what you mean. Ask the listener (unless it is your dog) if your explanation is clear to them or what questions they have. Although they won't have the full context, they will likely help you further clarify what you mean and give you practice in sharing your ideas too.

3. *Connect to the desired culture.* Look at your clarified list to see if you have expectations in all three areas, and ask yourself if these expectations align with and support the desired culture. If not, adjust them until they do.

4. *Distinguish between wants and needs.* Some of your expectations are things you need and some others might be things you want. Remember that these are different things, and you need to know the difference. Knowing the difference and leading with needs will get you the best results.

5. *Make time for a conversation.* Schedule time with that person to talk about these expectations. Let them know about the purpose of the conversation and encourage them to come prepared. If you're part of a hybrid team, that conversation may happen on a day when both parties are in the office. If that's not an option, or if time is of the essence, use webcams for these individual conversations to enhance the richness of the communication. Encourage them to bring their expectations of you to the table, and be clear about what you're hoping to learn from them.

6. *Have a real conversation.* Honest, two-way communication is critical to your success. A real conversation isn't dominated by one party or the other. As the leader, you risk doing too much of the talking, sharing too quickly, and dominating—whether you mean

to or not. Start by asking questions at the beginning to get the other person talking. Try to make this as much of an equal conversation as possible. Have this session face to face if you can, and if not, make sure you are using your webcams. Richness will increase trust and understanding. As a part of this conversation, make sure you

- *Share examples.* It is hard to build real understanding and agreement without examples. As you talk about an expectation, give real-life examples of what success looks like and doesn't.

- *Confirm expectations in both directions.* Remember this isn't just about what you expect of them, but what they want and need from you as well. Make sure you explore the lists both of you brought. Don't discount the role time zones play in planning this meeting. A good time for you might be when the other person is thinking more about picking the kids up from school or getting supper on the table. If it's really important, find a time that allows everyone to keep their focus and attention on what's important.

- *Look through the culture lens together.* Remember that one of the reasons you are doing this exercise is to create and support your culture. Together look at the expectations you are agreeing to and ask: If we do these things, are we moving closer to our desired culture?

- *Check for understanding.* Running through the list isn't enough. If your team member Joan is nodding, it doesn't necessarily mean she understands. Take the time to make sure you have mutual understanding. We started by saying you must be clear on the expectations. Making sure the other person is just as clear closes the loop and creates the outcome you are looking for.

7. *Create agreement.* There is a difference between "I understand what is expected" and "I am committed to doing it." Ultimately, we need the second statement to be true.

Expectations Run Both Directions

Remember that while you might initiate the conversation, your teammate may even be looking for guidance and clarity from you. You need to understand what their expectations are, too. Make sure both of you recognize that the goal is to create mutually clear expectations for both of you.

Understanding and Agreement Is the Goal

The goal is to make sure expectations are clear to everyone on the team. Yet, like in much of our daily communication, we focus too much on what we are saying, and not enough on whether the other person understands. We cannot overstate the fact that "Well, I told them," doesn't mean you have understanding and agreement. Until everyone understands the expectations, their power is greatly diminished. And once you reach an understanding, both parties must agree on those expectations. You may not love one of the expectations, but if you understand it, you're far more willing and able to agree to it. You agree on a common definition of success. It is the mutual agreement to move toward the expectations that creates success and defines the culture. If we align them with the desired culture, we have taken a major step in the direction of that desired future.

Don't Stop

This may seem like a lot of work. You must clarify the expectations for yourself and have conversations with everyone. If you are a leader with ten team members, the time you need to spend might seem daunting. Consider this an investment—the time investment will pay off as all the dimensions that we mentioned earlier improve. After you have agreement, these expectations become the basis for your coaching and support. As the world, and the work, shift and change, you will probably need to tweak the expectations. Once you initially set them, though, like the momentum of a moving object, it will be much easier to maintain agreement and understanding.

Expectations among Teammates

Everything you have just read was written from the perspective of leader to teammate because that's how most people think about those conversations. Yet this all applies to peer-to-peer expectation setting as well. The needs for clarity and agreement on expectations are just as important here as your work to build a team and culture where people want to work and can be successful.

The process for setting expectations with a peer largely follows what you've just read. But there are two important differences between leader/teammate and teammate/teammate expectations. With a leader there is a power differential that is not there with a peer. And let's face it, we don't usually think about these differences in power or status except with our boss.

When leaders give individuals the freedom, skills, and expectations to have these conversations, clearer expectations exist across the organization.

Final Thoughts

Clear working expectations are about more than the work itself and they apply to everyone. When we expand expectation setting beyond a leadership role and teammates to talk about what they want and need in their working environment, we create a new dynamic.

Understanding how flexible work impacts the balance of "real-time" communication and asynchronous messages on a hybrid team helps reduce the endless barrage of web meetings. Agreeing on when a meeting could have been an email has a long-term impact on how the team shares information and collaborates. Do not discount time and place as factors in creating a new way of working and connecting.

Although the expectations themselves are the foundation of creating your new culture, the open process of creating them between team members is a powerful shift too. Mastering this process will positively change your culture forever.

Chapter 12

Creating Team Agreements

Ahmed has worked with his team to build a cultural vision. The team seems on board. The vision seems clear, and he has adjusted his expectations with individual team members to align with the new vision. But he senses there's still something missing. The team isn't making as much progress as quickly as he had hoped. The initial momentum and energy for the new culture is waning and he is afraid much of the hard work may be lost. The fact that the team works at a distance seems to make it worse. He wonders what he did wrong, and what else he can do to help the team move toward the culture they jointly created.

By all accounts Ahmed and his team have done many things right. Remember that designing a team and refining a culture is managing change, and therefore, it can be hard. Progress may come in fits and starts. Even after you acknowledge that, something else might still be missing.

Even if Ahmed (or you) followed our process to create real engagement in and commitment to the future you envision, you are still the leader—people may still see it as your vision and your baby. People may feel ownership for the outcomes individually but feel powerless beyond their conversations and interaction with you as the leader.

What's missing?

Peer pressure.

Although we often associate peer pressure with being a negative thing (did your parents ever ask, "If everyone else was walking off the edge of the cliff would you?"), it can be a positive force too. If the team has agreed on the cultural vision (although we recognize some members may be more on the fence than others), positive peer pressure makes doing things differently cool and expected.

To get there, we need one more tool in our toolkit—team agreements. These agreements can reduce conflict and increase harmony and productivity, but they can also be used to drive behaviors associated with your aspirational culture.

Agreements versus Expectations

Team agreements are the final (for now) version of the expectations across a group. We've talked about why expectations between people are so powerful and how to create them. But the team is more than the sum of its parts.

Joe and Gina have clarified how they'll work together. So have Sue and Charlie, and all four have clear expectations with Ahmed their boss, but they haven't talked about how they will all work together. That is where team agreements come in.

We've noted that expectations will be successful when they are mutually clear and everyone understands and agrees. Similarly, team agreements are written statements of behavior that

- Create a common understanding and expectation of behaviors, processes, and interactions across the team

- Move the team toward the desired culture

- Allow each team member to accept and agree with them

Why They Help

We don't typically share what our boss expects of us with the rest of the team. How Joe and Gina work together is most important to them, but their expectations of each other don't really matter to the rest of the team. But behaviors and processes apply across the entire team too. If you stop at expectations, you may be suboptimizing. And as powerful as expectations are, you may miss larger issues or irritants.

On a long-distance team, the agreements may be what is missing in reinforcing the desired culture. Even if individual expectations are set and clear, some team interactions may be difficult or full-on dysfunctional. As much as we believe in the power of team agreements for any team, we believe they can be even more powerful for your remote, hybrid, or any kind of Long-Distance Team.

What Is Included

What might be included in your team agreements may vary widely. It will depend on the team's history, maturity, dynamics, location, and circumstances, as well as how far your current culture is from what you desire. Although this is not a complete list, here are some of the situations that you and your teammates might need to agree on:

- Both how we interact and the roles we play in meetings

- How often, when, and where we meet (for example, do we have hybrid meetings or wait until everyone is in the office?)

- Which communication tools we use and when (i.e., when do we use instant messaging [IM], email, or text? When do we call and/or leave voice mails?)

- How we communicate with the full team if some are in the office and some are full-time remote

- Accepted response times to emails or other communication

- How we hand work off from one part of the team to another

- The types of things we communicate to everyone so that one group doesn't feel like they are left out of the loop or that they always hear news last

- Who cleans the office refrigerator or does the dishes? What does it mean to the remote members of the team when those in the office concentrate on problems like this that don't directly impact them?

There are several things to note here. Notice the prevalence of meeting and communication questions. These factors affect the entire team. And for some of them, individual expectations could exist, yet team agreements will help. Gina and Suzy might agree to when they email versus IM, but if their agreement is different than Gina's and Charlie's, pretty soon we have a jumbled communication mess. If the team agrees that they will use an IM channel for certain communications, work is easier, clearer, and cleaner.

We're sure you noticed the last item on the list. It is a placeholder to make a point that team agreements can (and should) address the common irritants the cause friction and conflict on teams. It is hard to have a wonderful culture when people are upset about "little things." If you have ever had a small pebble in your shoe, you know what we mean; as small as it is, it can become the only thing we focus on. Why did we use the office kitchen as our example when we are focusing on remote teams? Because over the years, as we have facilitated sessions to create team agreements, office kitchen behavior nearly always makes the list. There may be little things like this on your remote or hybrid teams too; make sure you don't ignore or bypass those irritants.

Napoleon said, "To avoid war, you avoid the thousand little pinpricks that lead to war." On a remote team, those pinpricks might be as tiny as refusing to use your webcam when everyone else is on theirs, or sending an email to everyone rather than in a specific group chat. Little things matter more than we think they do (or should).

How to Create Formal Agreements

Creating team agreements isn't conceptually different than creating expectations. Basically,

- Everyone thinks about their wants and needs for their work.

- You come together to talk about those wants and needs.

- You come to agreement on things you can do and ways to work together that meet those needs.

But doing it with five, seven, or fourteen people is far more complex than doing it with one other person.

That's why we suggest a structured process to create agreements as a team. Here are the steps:

1. *Introduce the need and purpose for team expectations.* This chapter should give you what you need.

2. *Set a meeting to start.* Schedule a meeting for this purpose with no competing agenda items. It will likely take more than one meeting and some bumpy sessions, but you must start somewhere. State and expect that people come prepared for this meeting.

3. *Prepare by thinking about what you want and need from the rest of the team.* Everyone should do this work—not just the leader or whomever else might have called this meeting. Everyone should think about this as it relates to overall productivity and effectiveness and the desired culture. In other words, think about both the work itself and how we get it done. Individually answering these questions will help:

   - What frustrates me or diverts my focus and keeps me from being productive?

   - What could we do differently that would help us all?

   - What behaviors create barriers to relationships or the work?

   - What do I wish was different?

   - If I could wave my magic wand, what would I change?

   - What are the things we always complain about but never seem to change? (And how much better would things be if they did change?)

4. *Meet with a neutral facilitator.* We recommend the leader not facilitate this meeting. They should attend this meeting not as the leader, but as a member of the team. Having an outside facilitator will allow everyone to participate and minimize the impact of rank or positional power. If possible, have this meeting either with everyone in-person or everyone virtual; keeping the playing field level here is important to reaching understanding and final agreement.

5. *Share needs.* Have individuals share from their prework. Start with needs. Ask one person to share one of their items and see if others have something similar, then continue listing out a complete,

nonduplicated list. A whiteboard or flipchart (real or virtual, in your meeting platform) is a must.

6. *Map to the culture.* Once the list is shared and people understand the needs, map the list to the culture to make sure you have focused on needs that align with your cultural vision. Make sure that none of the agreements runs counter to or hinders you in reaching your desired culture.

7. *Talk about wants.* Wants are not the same as needs. Wants are preferences, and "wouldn't it be nice ifs." Once you have the collective list of needs and have considered the culture, ask if anyone has any wants for the group to consider.

8. *Draft agreements.* Start with something on the list that has lots of energy around it. Take that item and ask, What can we agree to do that will achieve or eliminate this? As the group talks, create a statement that reflects the behaviors/processes the team is thinking about. Frame it as follows: *We will reduce the amount of irrelevant email in our inboxes by using unique Slack channels to include only those with a real stake in that topic.* The statement starts with "we" and is behavioral and observable. The goal here isn't just to gain agreement for the behaviors, but to confirm that if we agree, we solve the issue or concern. Continue to work through your list translating each item into draft agreements.

9. *Provide time to think.* Once the team has the draft list, give them time to think about it. If you complete a draft list in one meeting, stop, and then schedule a follow-up meeting. Give people time to review the list and think about four important questions:

   ▪ If we do live up to these agreements, will we have a better, more effective working environment that matches our desired culture?

- If not, why not?

- Can I accept and agree to live these agreements?

- If not, why not?

10. *Finalize and document the agreements.* After people have had time to think and review, reconvene. In the interim, you can set up a channel in your IM tool to facilitate group discussion and clarifications. The power of these agreements come from each person saying to the rest of the group that they will accept and agree to these statements. To garner that power, we recommend that this be a synchronous meeting, regardless of where people are located. Go through each of the draft statements, asking each person to state to the rest of the group that they will accept and agree to live up to that statement. If each person does so, the agreement is finalized. If someone says they can't "accept and agree," they must say why. Then, with the help of the group, edit the agreement so that everyone can accept and agree. If you can't reach 100 percent agreement, the item doesn't make the list.

What if you can't reach agreement on something important? If you want engagement and ownership of the whole list, don't give up too soon—clarity is worth the wait and work. If something can't gain full agreement and you as the leader feels it is necessary, you can make it a full-group expectation, but avoid this if possible. An expectation of the leader won't carry the same power as peer pressure of an agreement. In our experience, your team will be able to come to valuable agreements, even if it takes some time.

Congratulations! At this point you have team agreements that can propel you collectively toward your vision. Beyond that, if you have used an open process, chances are team members understand, know, and trust each other more—and have a broader perspective on the needs and situations of team members too.

Want more examples? Although team agreements will be unique to your team, the statements should be succinct and mutually clear. After all, we can't agree to something we don't understand. We have some examples at LongDistanceTeamBook.com/agreements if that is helpful.

Creating Consequences

As in most situations there are two types of possible consequences related to these team agreements: positive ones and negative ones.

The positive consequences of teammates living up to these agreements are obvious—you will move predictably toward your desired culture and have less workplace conflict as a side benefit. But what if people don't live up to the agreements?

Your agreements will likely require everyone to change their approaches and routines, at least a bit. They'll also need an occasional reminder. When everyone is in the same boat, people will likely grant each other some grace as they grow into the agreements. And if someone needs some skills in order to live up to an agreement, the team will likely help. But what if someone consistently misses the mark?

Let's say that this is one of your agreements: *We agree to complete expected action items on time*, and as a team, you review action items at each meeting. If Wanda misses her due date once, she might have a good reason, and the team may accept it. But after the second meeting when she is late, and she knows she will have to report to the full team, chances are she will figure out how to proudly say "completed" at that meeting.

If appropriate peer pressure isn't enough, the leader can use this as a coaching opportunity. These agreements should be seen as a part of people's job performance, not an "extra." If Wanda is wonderful at her core job but isn't living up to these agreements, there is a real performance issue and it should be treated (and coached to) as such. Remember—culture is part of the work and belongs to everyone.

Final Thoughts

We can toss around the word *agreements,* but what we have talked about is something specific—agreements across a team. When time is invested to create these, you set the stage for reaching the culture you want, and helping everyone, including those who are remote, feel like a true part of the team.

Chapter 13

Creating Engagement

Li thought everything was fine. She and her team had painstakingly assessed how they did their work and had laid out a design plan that everyone—or at least it seemed to be everyone—bought into. The team aspires to be fun and informal, with a high degree of trust. Over the last few weeks, though, she's noticed some things in her one-on-one conversations with team members. There's more complaining about teammates and the need for more rework than before, which slows down the workflow. Was she wrong about the team's commitment or is the culture changing?

Culture never stops evolving because people constantly change. Some people thrive in the new structure; some are frustrated. Individual contributors leave and new people, with new ideas, come in. Someone who was happy coming into the office every day is now tired and stressed from the commute and wants to change their agreement. Maybe someone is struggling with one of their teammates. Everyone contributing to a project feels slow, and someone decides, "It's easier to ask for forgiveness than permission."

The goal with a team's culture is to have it morph along the lines you aspire to, not take on a life of its own. For this to happen, both the leader and the individual teammates have to pay attention to what's happening and choose to act in ways that support that vision. They need to believe in the aspirational goals and choose to act in ways that support it.

In other words, they need to be engaged.

The frustrating thing for Li and leaders like her, is that there's only so much the organization, senior leadership, and the team leader can do. True engagement is individual.

Think about this personal example. You find someone you want to get to know better. You take them out, spend time with them, get them to like you, and decide you want to commit to them. You buy a ring, get down on one knee, and ask them to marry you. You've done all you can. You aren't engaged until they say yes.

One of the great frustrations of leadership is that you can't make people engage at work. Certainly, organizations and leaders can create an environment in which people choose to give discretionary effort, act for the good of the team, and go the extra mile for their teammates. Heaven knows, they can also do things that motivate people to act in the completely opposite way. The ultimate choice belongs to the individual.

There are some important reasons people don't make the choice to engage. Two of the biggest are that they don't know they can (it's work after all), or they think it just means "do more work."

Some people have grown up with a vision of work as a necessary evil. When they hear people talk about being engaged at work, they look at those people like they have three heads. Sure, it seems like a good idea, but is it even possible? Leaders need to remember that not everyone thinks of their jobs the same way. That difference often accounts for why the manager was promoted in the first place.

One other question must be asked here: Can people be engaged (or remain engaged) when working alone or largely at a distance from their teammates? In our experience, both personally and with clients, the answer is absolutely yes! When leaders and team members understand the nature and benefits that engagement brings, they are more likely to make that choice. Leaders need to pay attention to different factors (that we will discuss in this chapter) and can't rely on fluffy in-office gambits like dry cleaning services, ping pong tables, or comfy chairs—those aren't really the answer anyway.

Why Would Anyone Choose Engagement?

Think about a time when you were engaged in your work. Think about how that felt for you. Chances are some or all these things were true. You were

- Enjoying your work more

- Seeing how your work was contributing to something meaningful or important

- Building stronger relationships with those you worked with

- Seeing chances to make a bigger difference—and maybe earn recognition or a promotion

- Increasing your productivity

- Providing discretionary effort—because you want to

- Getting noticed

Who doesn't want those things?

The Leader's Role

This doesn't absolve leaders of responsibility. Here are some things the organization and the leader can do to create an environment where people choose to engage positively:

- Help people see the value of engagement.

- Ensure people understand the vision.

- Listen to the team to identify disconnects with that vision.

- Lead, coach, and offer feedback with your desired culture in mind.

- Model engagement yourself.

Employee engagement is voluntary, and conscious. People choose to engage with their work, or not, and they make multiple decisions each day that confirm their commitment or lead them down another path. As a leader (with positional authority or not) you can influence that decision.

Help People See the Value of Engagement

Let's face it, people might see "engagement" as "they just want more work out of me," but when you ask people if they want the things on the preceding list, most people will eagerly say yes. People don't even have to want the whole list—one bullet point might change their view of work, their role in it, and their engagement choice. Once people see benefits to them (not just the organization) for choosing to engage, you are well on the way.

In fact, when people are working from home, they may value engagement even more as they may be more isolated in other areas of life without the social benefits they might have gotten in an office setting.

Ensure People Understand the Vision

You've had the meeting. You've discussed the plan with your people and had multiple conversations where everyone said they "got it." So why do we have to keep harping on the subject? Whether we are talking about the culture or overall business objectives, the point is the same. We can get so caught up in the task list that we lose sight of the big picture. We're like McLuhan's fish—too busy swimming to know we're in water.

It's not that people necessarily disagree or choose to act counter to the culture you all envisioned; they just aren't thinking about it like you are.

The good news is that you should have plenty of support in your effort. When you and your colleagues designed the team, you produced plenty of documentation. You clearly defined and articulated goals. You should have plans and agreements in writing to refer to and share with the team.

Kevin is very conscious of the big picture and culture at the Kevin Eikenberry Group. As a result, in every full team meeting, he starts by reviewing our Mission, Vision, and Values and closes with a statement of how we will approach work. It's not exactly our "culture statement," because it also encompasses some external items, but it has similarities and might help you get started.

We will

- Be positive and proactive—internally and externally.

- Be nonpolitical.

- Be creative.

- Be aggressive.

- Be empathetic.

- Double down on being the trusted advisor/resource.

- Be a model hybrid team.

He doesn't spend a lot of time rehashing this list—after all, we talk about it each month—but none of the team members can claim they aren't aware of what our desired culture is. As much as human beings can, we model those behaviors, and it's a pretty good window into what it's like to work here.

Wayne will confess that the periodic reminder does occasionally force him to adjust his behavior. He could be more positive, and certainly less political. A little reminder keeps him in alignment with the team.

As new people join the team, this is an early part of the interview discussion. People need to know what they are getting into when they come work here. By the time they are hired, they know what it will be like to work with us. It's impossible for people to meet expectations if they don't know what those expectations are. Even when they do, they may need an occasional reminder.

Listen to Identify Disconnects

Leaders know that it's easier to correct, or adjust to, behavior when it first occurs. One of the reasons people believe that managing was easier when everyone was in the same location was that you could actually see and hear how people interacted every day. This gave you the chance (though it wasn't always taken) to correct something before it became a bad habit. The team's culture was on display each day. When we work apart from each other, even part time, we don't get the same obvious clues about what's going on with people.

A particular challenge with looking and listening for problems or behaviors that don't match the desired culture, is that, in the words of the great detective, Hercule Poirot, "You are looking for what isn't there."

Remember that on remote and hybrid teams, some of the most corrosive behaviors are exclusion and self-isolation. The problem isn't that you hear people complaining . . . it's that you don't hear them at all.

When people stop making themselves heard or seen, it's a good bet that they've disengaged. It might be because they feel excluded from the work the rest of the team is doing. Maybe they have something going on in their personal lives that makes work less of a priority. There could be multiple reasons people stop acting in a way that supports the team's desired culture. It could be temporary, in which case it will pass, or chronic, which means it is more serious and requires your attention.

Leaders should be looking out for these signs that people are disengaged from the work of the team:

- *Changes in how people communicate.* Have people stopped responding to emails and group chats? When you ask for input or feedback, have certain people gone silent?

- *Changes in how people interact with their teammates, particularly in meetings.* Are people who've always been active participants suddenly sitting silently? Maybe they're reluctant to use their webcams or must be prompted for their opinions or feedback?

- *Missed deadlines and decreased work quality.* Have good performers suddenly experienced a decrease in productivity and effectiveness?

- *Changes in proactivity.* Have people stopped volunteering for tasks? Do you need to specifically ask people to help where they used to just step up?

There's one more important way to hear if people's level of engagement has changed—ask them. That leads us to the next, and perhaps most important, way to gauge engagement.

Lead, Coach, and Offer Feedback

The best opportunity to listen to your employees is during a conversation with them. If you get the sense that something is up—that they are disengaged or are behaving in ways that don't support the rest of the team—it's your job as the leader to be curious and learn more.

The best way to ensure people know how to demonstrate their engagement and commitment to the team's culture is to model it ourselves. If we act in accordance with expectations, people will take their cues from the leader. They always have.

When engaging in coaching conversations or one-on-ones, you can hear what's happening with people. Listen actively and be on the lookout for words or phrases that indicate something isn't right.

Here are some things to listen for:

- Repeated use of "I" instead of "we" when referring to the team's work.

- Reluctance to expand on thinking. Even when you ask open-ended questions, people seem hesitant to speak or give detailed answers.

- Terms of resignation such as, "whatever," or "I don't care." Especially listen for safe but misleading terms like "fine."

When leading coaching conversations, it is important to do more listening than speaking. As we have mentioned many times in previous books, give the team member the chance to speak first; they should do at least 51 percent of the talking.

Listen carefully, and don't be afraid to ask follow-up questions. One of the most powerful things you can ask is "Why do you say that?" You'll be surprised at what you learn, and you may not like some of it. Even so, it may be what you need to know, and it may give you a chance to be encouraging and help people choose to re-engage.

Model Engagement Yourself

As a leader you are a role model; people are watching what you do and say. Are you engaged? Do you care about the work and the people? Are you willing to go the extra mile, not because you have to, but because you want to? Do you find passion and meaning in your work?

What do they see in you that gives them that impression? Ralph Waldo Emerson said, "Your actions speak so loudly, I can't hear what you say." Remember, your intentions are important, but people judge you (and everyone) by what they see and hear, not what's intended.

If you want your team members to choose engagement, your example is the most persuasive arrow in your quiver.

Be Aware of the Balance

Engagement is great—and everyone benefits from it. But there needs to be a limit. Team members who want to be noticed, especially if working remotely, might feel that volunteering for everything and answering emails and taking meetings anytime will be seen as a positive. And leaders are often high achievers and are especially excited about their work; that might be why they were promoted.

Can we be highly engaged, with all the personal and organization benefits that come with it, and still have a life?

We can, and while the balance might be different for different people and different times in life, that balance is critical. Good leaders model engagement, great leaders model a solid work/life balance—because that is what they need from their teams too.

Is It One or Many?

If you determine there is a lack of engagement, ask yourself this question: *Is this isolated to one person or is it an epidemic?*

If it is just the individual, probe to uncover the source of the disengagement. Almost nobody is committed to the team 100 percent of the time. We have bad days and slumps in our motivation and behavior. A kind word, a reminder about the value they bring to their work and how important they are, and a reminder of the aspirational culture will help.

If there's a specific challenge, do what's in your power as the team leader to assist. They might need training, or they might need to have a discussion with another teammate that you can facilitate. If there's something in their personal life that's interfering with their work, do what you can to accommodate their needs.

If the disengagement is more widespread, it might be time to raise the issue with the team. Again, the leader needs to speak less and listen more. Also, consider asynchronous and anonymous ways to check the mood of the team, rather than calling everyone together for a meeting to "hash things out." Besides, you aren't trying to "fix" them; you want to understand why they aren't choosing to engage and see what you can do to help them change their choice.

If there seems to be a serious problem with the culture of the team, get to the root cause. It's possible your team design needs to be reexamined or you might be able to address external factors.

Let's say personnel changes made since the team was put together have impacted the culture in unexpected ways. Is it reasonable to expect the new people to just "get with the program," or is it time to reexamine and assess the team design and set new goals?

Whatever the reason people disengage, the worst thing a leader or teammate can do is ignore it and hope the problem goes away. It seldom does, and often it spreads to other members of the team. Although none of us like to be miserable, misery loves company.

Engagement comes from inside that person, but it doesn't mean there's nothing leaders and teammates can do to help people choose to engage with their work, the team, and the aspirational culture.

Final Thoughts

Engagement is more than a score on a survey and is certainly more than an action item for leaders. Engagement is an individual choice that can be supported by leaders and teammates. When you apply the ideas and mindsets we've discussed, the odds are that your team's true engagement and commitment will grow.

Conclusion

We said at the beginning of this book that we're not creating a post-Covid roadmap. However, the pandemic gave us pause and will lead to new ways of thinking about designing and redesigning teams. We hope this book is a useful part of those efforts.

In particular, the rise of hybrid work challenges assumptions about how teams work, how people collaborate, and what makes for a great culture. It's tempting to think we can take this moment in time, design or redesign our team, create or maintain our aspirational culture, and then just get on with the work.

It's tempting, but wrong.

Work constantly evolves around us. The work we do and the way we interact with each other will continue to change. Team members leave and are replaced by new people with a different set of skills, assumptions, and talent. Technology alters how we work with each other, and even the nature of the work may change over time.

Additionally, we get older and our personal circumstances change. What is important to someone worrying about childcare is less important to empty-nesters. Someone's engagement level early in their career may be vastly different than the same person's engagement when they are nearing retirement. Relationships can strengthen, but they also can fracture or disintegrate. We're human. As many factors impact our team design and culture as there are members of your team.

Even if nothing external changes, it's human nature to fall back on old habits or thought patterns. Just because people buy into working and pledge to work in a certain way, there's no guarantee they will continue to be engaged, motivated, and mindful of how they work with each other in the future.

From time to time, it is important to assess your team's design and culture. The good news is you now have the resources to make that job easier and less stressful. Whenever you need to, you can go back to the concepts we've discussed and take another look at what's happening whenever it is needed.

We set out to create a way for you to

- Assess (or reassess) your team design and culture.

- Identify gaps between your aspirations and what everyone's encountering each day.

- Engage your team in reconnecting to those lofty goals.

- Coach your team on the behaviors and mindsets necessary to sustain the culture.

- Keep yourself on track.

Most importantly, now if you find your design isn't creating the culture you want, you know what to do about it.

Building teams and cultures (either macro or micro) is not easy. Whether you're a senior leader, a team leader, or an individual trying to lead by example, it takes a lot of thought, discipline, and skill.

With the *Long-Distance Leader, Long-Distance Teammate,* and now the *Long-Distance Team,* our mission has been to help leaders at all levels of all organizations. When you use these together, you have the resources, support, and inspiration to design, work in, and lead a terrific team that can overcome the challenges of distance and hybrid work.

Like all our "Long-Distance" books, we've set up online resources for this book that will help you. You can find them all at LongDistanceTeam-Book.com.

If you want to talk about what's going on in your organization, or need extra assistance, reach out to us at The Kevin Eikenberry Group. Regardless, we wish you all success in your mission to build a successful, collaborative, and high-energy Long-Distance Team.

Acknowledgments

This is the first book we've written since going through the Covid-19 experience. We would be wrong not to acknowledge that many of the lessons in this book come directly from the experiences of our colleagues, customers, and friends. This has been a crazy, stressful time, but in all such historical eras people have had opportunities to learn and grow. Because we don't want to waste any experience, we thank them all for the lessons they've learned and shared with us.

We try not to make our work theoretical; instead we ground it in what we know works. For many of these lessons, we look to our teammates and colleagues at the Kevin Eikenberry Group who continue to teach us what commitment, hard work, and a little humor can accomplish. We also have to thank our families for their support, love, and understanding. Finally, the team at Berrett-Koehler continues to be a great role model for creative partnering in a virtual world. Trust, innovation, and connection are possible regardless of geography—our relationship with them as our publisher is one more example of this for us.

From Kevin

After I'm introduced to a group with a list of some of my accomplishments, books I've authored, and more, I mention that the most important thing the group should know is that I am leading every day. I believe that doing the work of leading keeps me grounded and makes our work—including this book—more effective and valuable. Leading for over twenty-five years, and doing it at a distance for far over a decade, has given me examples and ideas and challenges me to practice what we teach. None of this is possible without our remarkable team of rockstars at The Kevin Eikenberry Group, past and present. I thank you all.

Certainly, the lessons and insights come from our customers and colleagues—and the list of all of them is far too long to print, so I won't. You know who you are. Each of you is treasured. Without you, there wouldn't be a Kevin Eikenberry Group.

In my book *Remarkable Leadership*, I wrote something like this: *As we become better leaders, we become better human beings—and vice versa.* That is my way of connecting personal and professional development together. More specifically, it is from my family that I continue to learn how to be a better human, leader, trainer, and author. All my love and thanks go to Lori, Parker, and Kelsey, but also to Mom, Marisa, Lori's family, and all my extended family.

Lastly, I thank my Lord and Savior, who has granted me grace, love, forgiveness, and the blessing to do the work He placed me on this planet to do.

From Wayne

I am fortunate to have worked at least partly remote, or had remote teammates, for my entire career. My work life began at the same time email started, allowing people to work from anywhere, and I've been fascinated by the changes this has made in the workplace and the world at large. It's been my honor to document these and help people make sense of the new environment.

The work we do, and the lessons I've learned from it, are not theoretical. My colleagues and customers continue to inspire, surprise, and energize me. I am grateful for all of you.

What hasn't changed during this time is the love and support of my family. Not just The Duchess and Her Serene Highness, but my family in Canada. Strong, loving, remote connections are not just reserved for the workplace.

Index

A

accountability, 80, 121
Ag Alumni Seed, 44
agreements
  and expectations, 115, 121, 134–135
  voting, 78
  see also team agreements
Ahmed (manager), 137
Alice (team leader), 83
aspirational culture
  defined, 94
  measurement in, 123–124
  nurturing, 114–115
  refining, 121–123
  reinforcing, 116–118, 139, 151–152
  and skills, 118–121
  see also culture redefinition
assessments
  of 3C Model dimensions, 57–59
  of culture, 35
  of culture creation, 31
  of engagement, 123, 152–153,
    153–156
  see also measurements
asynchronous meetings, 75–77

B

behaviors
  aspirational, 116–117
  and culture, 4, 18–19, 147–148
  issues, 137–138, 145–146,
    155–156
  modelling, 30–31, 34, 35–36
beliefs
  and culture, 18
  and engagement, 148
brainstorming sessions, 77–78
breakout rooms, 75

C

Carey (team leader), 113
chat technologies, 76–77
Cho (new teammate), 25
coaching, 33–34, 80, 154
cohesion
  assessments, 58–59
  dimensions, 54–56
  in team design, 71
collaboration
  assessments, 58
  paradigms and opportunities, 52–54

collaboration *(continued)*
  in team design, 70
commitment vs. compliance, 64–66
communications
  as 3C model dimension, 49–52
  agreements on, 139–140
  assessments, 57–58
  of culture and values, 29, 102
  decline of, 153
  in team design, 70
  written, 76–77
competence, 74
compliance vs. commitment, 64–66
conflicts, 129, 140–141
contractors, 97
culture
  assessments, 35
  and behavior, 147–148
  characteristics, 4, 20
  examples, 18–19
  micro vs. macro, 21
  see also aspirational culture;
    macroculture; microculture
culture creation
  assessments, 31
  communication of, 29
  individual responsibility for, 34–38
  and middle managers, 32–33
  and senior leadership, 26–29, 30–31
  and systems, 29–30
  and team dynamic, 33–34
  and team leaders, 31–32
culture redefinition, 93–103
  draft vision, 99–101
  finalization and communication, 102
  gathering feedback, 101–102
  process overview, 95–96
  recruiting team for, 97–99
  senior leadership in, 93–94
  timing and justification, 96–97

D

decision-making and culture, 115,
  121–123
documentation
  inclusivity in, 76–77
  team agreements, 144
  team design plan, 79–80

E

Eikenberry, Kevin, 21, 27–28, 151–152
  The Long-Distance Leader (with
    Turmel), 1, 2, 43, 47–48
  The Long-Distance Teammate (with
    Turmel), 1, 47–48
engagement
  assessments, 123, 152–153, 153–156
  in culture redefinition, 97
  maintaining, 160
  modelling, 154–155
  motivations for, 149, 150
  in team design, 81–82
  in workplace culture, 147–149
expectations
  areas of, 130–131
  and culture, 117–118, 129–130
  and performance excellence, 80
  and psychological safety, 74
  role of, 127–129
  setting, 131–134
  vs. team agreements, 138–139

F

facilitators, 72, 74, 98, 142
failures, 30–31
fish in water analogy, 35, 40, 151
flexible teams, 15
flowcharts, 76

H

Human Resources (HR), 119, 124

hybrid teams
  defined, 15
  designing, 48
    and microculture, 36, 105, 112, 121, 122
hybridization analogy, 44–45

I

inclusion strategies, 76, 78
independent teams, 13–14
influences
  of leaders, 36–37
  of systems, 29–30
interdependent teams, 13–14

J

Julia (new leader), 17
Julio (leader), 47

K

knowledge work, 40–41
Kris (project manager), 9, 11

L

language diversity, 76
leadership
  culturally appropriate behaviors, 34–38
  and decision-making, 121–123
  power differentials, 73, 144
  in team design co-creation, 64–66, 72–73, 82
  and team engagement, 150, 153–156
  and workplace paradigms, 39–41, 148
  see also middle managers; senior leadership; team leaders
Learning and Development (L&D), 119
Li (team leader), 147
Long-Distance Leader, The (Eikenberry and Turmel), 1, 2, 43, 47–48

Long-Distance Teammate, The (Eikenberry and Turmel), 1, 47–48
Long-Distance Teams
  culture reinforcement, 34, 122, 139
  defined, 15
  and workplace engagement, 86, 149
Luisa (team leader), 105

M

macroculture
  vs. microculture, 21
  and microculture alignment, 25, 33, 109, 110–111
  skills development for, 119
Malcolm (seasoned leader), 39
mappings
  agreements to culture, 143
  work to team, 80
McLuhan, Marshall, fish in water analogy, 35, 40, 151
measurements, 115, 123–124
meetings
  discussion guidelines, 81, 102
  with full team, 77–79
  interactions in, 153
  logistics, 75–77
  in team agreement development, 141–143
  see also asynchronous meetings; synchronous meetings
microculture
  of hybrid teams, 121
  vs. macroculture, 21
  and macroculture alignment, 25, 33, 109, 110–111
microculture change, 105–112
  creating vision, 108–111
  finalizing and operationalizing, 111–112
  planning for, 105–106

microculture change *(continued)*
    recruiting team for, 108
    timing and justification, 107–108
micromanagement, 129
middle managers, 32–33
mission statements, 81, 151
models
    3P Model of Remote-Work Success,
        47–48
    remote working, 41–42
    Three O Model of Leadership, 43–44
    see also 3C Model for Team and
        Culture Design
motivation
    and commitment, 65
    and trust, 74
    understanding leaders', 39–40

N

NPS (Net Promoter Score), 31

O

offices *see* workplaces
organization charts, 76

P

peer pressure, 138, 144
performance
    expectations, 80
    workplace, 9–10
power differentials, 73, 144
project managers *see* team leaders
psychological safety, 72, 73–74
purpose, 74

R

Rajesh (manager), 63
recordings, 77, 102
remote teams
    and culture, 36–37, 112

defined, 15
    workplace engagement, 149
remote working model, 41–42, 47–48
resources, 160–161

S

Sara (middle manager), 127
senior leadership
    and culture creation, 26–29
    in culture redefinition, 93–94
skills development, 115, 118–121
Slack, 76, 79
Stephano (CEO), 93
stories and culture, 18–19
synchronous meetings, 74–75
systems, 29–30

T

team agreements, 137–146
    creation, 141–145
    enforcement, 145–146
    vs. expectations, 138–139
    scope, 139–141
team design
    constraints, 83–84
    overview, 63–64
    requirements, 3–4
team design co-creation
    accountability, 80–82
    deliverables, 71
    documentation, 79–80
    dream design questions, 66–71
    guidelines, 64–66, 72–73, 74–75
    information gathering, 75–77
    team meeting process, 77–79
team leaders, 31–32
team redesign, 83–89
    membership assessment, 85–86
    process, 83–84, 89
    structure and constraints, 87–89

teammates
 and engagement, 147–148, 155–156
 expectations among, 135
 new, 25, 33–34, 152
teams
 composition, 43
 creation challenges, 9–13
 culture dynamic in, 33–34
 in culture redefinition, 97–99
 skill development in, 120–121
 types, 13–14, 15–16
 see also hybrid teams; Long-Distance
  Teams; remote teams
Teams (Microsoft), 76, 79
technologies
 agreements on, 140
 for documentation, 79
 for meetings, 75–77, 78
 skills development in, 119
The Kevin Eikenberry Group, 27–28, 37,
  81, 119, 151–152
Three O Model of Leadership, 43–44
3C Model for Team and Culture Design
 assessments with, 57–59
 and culture redefinition, 100
 and expectations, 131
 pillars, 48–56, 59–60
 and team redesign, 88–89
 uses, 56
3P Model of Remote-Work Success, 47–48
trust, 74, 121, 128
Turmel, Wayne, 28, 30, 152
 The Long-Distance Leader (with
  Eikenberry), 1, 2, 43, 47–48
 The Long-Distance Teammate (with
  Eikenberry), 1, 47–48

U
Undercover Boss (TV series), 27

V
values, 19, 29, 81
Virtual Instructor Led Trainings
  (VILTs), 120
virtual meetings, 75–77
vision
 in aspirational culture, 99–101
 in microculture change, 108–111
 statements, 81
voting, 78–79

W
webcams, 78, 119, 120, 132, 133
whiteboards, 53, 143
work
 agreements and expectations, 129,
  130–131, 140, 142
 changing nature of, 1–2, 159
 decline in quality, 153
 and life balance, 155
 paradigms, 40–42, 148
 and team design vs. culture, 3–5
work locations, 9, 42
work processes, 42–43
work weeks, 40–42
workplaces
 co-located, 36
 conflicts in, 129, 140–141
 engagement in, 149
 performance in, 9–10
 team agreements in, 139–140

About the Authors

Kevin Eikenberry

Kevin Eikenberry is a recognized world expert on leadership development and learning and is the Chief Potential Officer of The Kevin Eikenberry Group (KevinEikenberry.com). In the last thirty years he has worked with leaders from fifty-three countries and organizations around the world.

Twice he has been named by Inc.com as one of the Top 100 Leadership and Management Experts in the world and Global Gurus lists him as #22 in a list of leadership thought leaders. He is the author, coauthor, or a contributing author to nearly twenty books, including *Remarkable Leadership, From Bud to Boss* (with Guy Harris), *The Long-Distance Leader* (with Wayne Turmel), and *The Long-Distance Teammate* (with Wayne Turmel). You can learn more about him, his blog, his podcast, and more at KevinEikenberry.me.

He is proud of his work and results but prouder and more blessed by the team he gets to work with each day and the customers they serve.

Wayne Turmel

For twenty-five years, Wayne Turmel has been fascinated by how people communicate—or don't—at work. He's spent the last sixteen years focused on the changing world of remote work and virtual communication. He does not just study it but lives it every day by leading remote teams as well as by working from home and elsewhere.

Wayne's work in the field has been recognized internationally. Marshall Goldsmith has called him "one of the most unique voices in leadership."

Wayne is the author or coauthor of fourteen books including the first two of the Long-Distance Worklife series, *The Long-Distance Leader* and *The Long-Distance Teammate,* as well as others on virtual communication and remote learning; he's even written five novels.

He lives, teaches, and writes from his home in Las Vegas.

Helping Remote Leaders and Their Teams Succeed

We're confident you found this book helpful, but we also know that it was just the tip of the iceberg. There's more to learn, and the Kevin Eikenberry Group is here to help. Our website gives you

More tools. Our award-winning blog shares the latest thinking on the continually evolving picture of the remote working world and is a source of leadership knowledge to help you to recognize your own potential and make a bigger positive difference in the world.

More learning opportunities. We offer a variety of learning opportunities for both leaders and anyone working remotely, from the unique design of "12 Weeks to Becoming a Great Remote Teammate" to the complete "Remote Leadership Certificate Series," to live, virtually delivered learning events, to on-demand offerings and e-learning tools to place on your organization's Learning Management System.

More help. If you want to talk about the broader organizational needs related to remote leadership and remote work, please reach out to us. You can find all this and more at KevinEikenberry.com. While you're there, be sure to use promo code BOOK to receive a 25 percent discount on any of our learning products.

For all the tools available to you as a reader of this book, go to LongDistanceTeamBook.com.

More than leading at a distance. This book has helped you think about the challenges and opportunities of working at a distance, but you likely have other challenges, needs, and questions. Since 1993, The Kevin Eikenberry Group has existed to help leaders and their teams become more effective, confident, and successful.

Helping senior leaders. Need an outside perspective to reach your business goals and objectives? We help senior leaders succeed through executive coaching and consultation on building a leadership pipeline, leading macroculture change, and conducting change initiatives.

Helping new and frontline leaders. Do you need support for your new or first-line leaders? We know their challenges, opportunities, and pain, and we help hundreds of these leaders grow each year. Through our Bud to Boss resources, we offer organizational and individual options to help your new and frontline leaders succeed.

Helping all leaders. Are you looking to build your skills and confidence as a leader whether you are new or have been doing this for a long time? We help all leaders with a wide variety of learning opportunities and coaching options.

Inspiring and informing teams and individuals. Are you looking for tools and options to help everyone in your organization engage and grow? We offer free tools, videos, podcasts, and much more to help all employees do so.

Learn more at KevinEikenberry.com.

Also by Kevin Eikenberry and Wayne Turmel

The Long-Distance Leader
Rules for Remarkable Remote Leadership

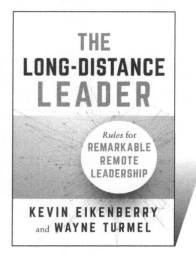

As more organizations adopt a remote workforce, the challenges of leading at a distance become more urgent than ever. The cofounders of the Remote Leadership Institute, Kevin Eikenberry and Wayne Turmel, show leaders how to guide their teams by recalling the foundational principles of leadership. The authors' "Three-O" Model refocuses leaders to think about outcomes, others, and ourselves—elements of leadership that remain unchanged, whether employees are down the hall or halfway around the world. By pairing it with the Remote Leadership Model, which emphasizes using technology as a tool and not a distraction, leaders are now able to navigate the terrain of managing teams wherever they are. Filled with exercises that ensure projects stay on track, keep productivity and morale high, and build lasting relationships, this book is the go-to guide for leading, no matter where people work.

Paperback, ISBN 978-1-5230-9461-5
PDF ebook, ISBN 978-1-5230-9462-2
ePub ebook, ISBN 978-1-5230-9463-9
Digital audio, ISBN 978-1-5230-9460-8

BK® Berrett–Koehler Publishers, Inc.
www.bkconnection.com   **800.929.2929**

Berrett–Koehler
Publishers

Berrett-Koehler is an independent publisher dedicated to an ambitious mission: *Connecting people and ideas to create a world that works for all.*

Our publications span many formats, including print, digital, audio, and video. We also offer online resources, training, and gatherings. And we will continue expanding our products and services to advance our mission.

We believe that the solutions to the world's problems will come from all of us, working at all levels: in our society, in our organizations, and in our own lives. Our publications and resources offer pathways to creating a more just, equitable, and sustainable society. They help people make their organizations more humane, democratic, diverse, and effective (and we don't think there's any contradiction there). And they guide people in creating positive change in their own lives and aligning their personal practices with their aspirations for a better world.

And we strive to practice what we preach through what we call "The BK Way." At the core of this approach is *stewardship,* a deep sense of responsibility to administer the company for the benefit of all of our stakeholder groups, including authors, customers, employees, investors, service providers, sales partners, and the communities and environment around us. Everything we do is built around stewardship and our other core values of *quality, partnership, inclusion,* and *sustainability.*

This is why Berrett-Koehler is the first book publishing company to be both a B Corporation (a rigorous certification) and a benefit corporation (a for-profit legal status), which together require us to adhere to the highest standards for corporate, social, and environmental performance. And it is why we have instituted many pioneering practices (which you can learn about at www.bkconnection.com), including the Berrett-Koehler Constitution, the Bill of Rights and Responsibilities for BK Authors, and our unique Author Days.

We are grateful to our readers, authors, and other friends who are supporting our mission. We ask you to share with us examples of how BK publications and resources are making a difference in your lives, organizations, and communities at www.bkconnection.com/impact.

Dear reader,

Thank you for picking up this book and welcome to the worldwide BK community! You're joining a special group of people who have come together to create positive change in their lives, organizations, and communities.

What's BK all about?

Our mission is to connect people and ideas to create a world that works for all.

Why? Our communities, organizations, and lives get bogged down by old paradigms of self-interest, exclusion, hierarchy, and privilege. But we believe that can change. That's why we seek the leading experts on these challenges—and share their actionable ideas with you.

A welcome gift

To help you get started, we'd like to offer you a **free copy** of one of our bestselling ebooks:

www.bkconnection.com/welcome

When you claim your **free ebook**, you'll also be subscribed to our blog.

Our freshest insights

Access the best new tools and ideas for leaders at all levels on our blog at ideas.bkconnection.com.

Sincerely,

Your friends at Berrett-Koehler

Certified

Corporation